SpringerBriefs in Econor

For further volumes:
http://www.springer.com/series/8876

Wilfried Ver Eecke

Ethical Reflections on the Financial Crisis 2007/2008

Making Use of Smith, Musgrave and Rajan

 Springer

Wilfried Ver Eecke
Georgetown University
Washington, DC
USA

ISSN 2191-5504   ISSN 2191-5512   (electronic)
ISBN 978-3-642-35090-0   ISBN 978-3-642-35091-7   (eBook)
DOI 10.1007/978-3-642-35091-7
Springer Heidelberg New York Dordrecht London

Library of Congress Control Number: 2012953564

Printed on acid-free paper

Springer is part of Springer Science+Business Media (www.springer.com)

For my grandchildren,
Maya, Josie, Michael, Eddy, Charlie, Ellie,
Emilie, Rogan, Preston, and Teagan,
who have such different personalities and
who surprise me so often with their
wonderful and spontaneous questions

Acknowledgments

I wish to thank Christian Rice for helping me to improve both the style and the ideas of the whole manuscript. I wish to thank Kate Henningsen who provided help both with the substance and the style of Chap. 3 ever since she was my research assistant with a GUROP grant. I also wish to thank my colleague, Professor George Brenkert, for his many suggestions, which allowed me to strengthen the argumentation, particularly in the latter part of Chap. 4.

I am grateful for the help received for writing Chap. 4 from Paul Duran, formerly from the IMF. An earlier version of this chapter was published as an article in Polish in 2012 in the *Quarterly Ethos*. I am happy to have received the permission from *Quarterly Ethos* to publish in English the Polish version of Chap. 4.

I am also grateful to Purdue University Press for giving me the permission to borrow with adaptation from the "Introduction" to *An Anthology Regarding Merit Goods. The Unfinished Ethical Revolution in Economic Thought*, 2007. West Lafayette, IN: Purdue University Press for writing Chap. 2.

This manuscript could not have been finished without the constant support of my wife, Josiane.

Contents

Chapter 1
Introduction

Abstract In this introduction I sketch the problem that I will address in the book: the financial crisis 2007–2008 and the subsequent recession. I point to the fact that notwithstanding Adam Smith's defense of the free market, he also points to a role for the government in promoting a well-functioning economy. I quote Adam Smith's argument for the necessity of governmental oversight of banking. We contrast this to Greenspan's naive belief in self-regulation of the banking system. We document Greenspan's opposition to banking regulation.

Keywords Adam Smith • Financial Crisis 2007–2008 • Banking regulations • Greenspan • Merit goods • Capitalism • The new economy

In this book I want to reflect on the philosophical bases of the financial crisis 2007–2008 and its subsequent recession. We will start with a close reading of Adam Smith's *An Inquiry into the Nature and Causes of the Wealth of Nations*. In that book we can see Smith's great admiration for the almost miraculous productivity of capitalism, the new economy. Smith then goes on to prove that this great productivity is the result of two factors; First, the new economy lets an individual free to pursue his or her own interest and so argues Smith, in intending his or her own gain "he is in this, as in many other case, led by an invisible hand to produce an end which was no part of his intention" (423).

Second, the new economy eliminates the government's intervention and management of the economy as was done before Smith's time in the Mercantile or Physiocratic economic systems. Adam Smith hereby articulates the two ideas that he is remembered for: in a free competitive economy self-interest produces good results and government intervention produces inefficiencies.

Adam Smith also observes that there are such economic goods as transportation facilities (roads) and education. Making use of modern economic theorizing, we see that Adam Smith is willing to affirm that his analysis of the new competitive economy applies only to that part of the economy consisting of private goods. Adam Smith then argues that a different kind of reasoning needs to apply for managing roads and education. For managing roads Smith introduces principles which are now more fully developed under the theory of public goods. For managing education Smith introduces principles which are now discussed under the theory of merit goods.

W. Ver Eecke, *Ethical Reflections on the Financial Crisis 2007/2008*,
SpringerBriefs in Economics, DOI: 10.1007/978-3-642-35091-7_1,
© The Author(s) 2013

Adam Smith articulates well the logic of optimal provision of private goods. We feel that the logic of optimal provision of public goods needs more elaboration. We do that in chapter two. We think that the problems connected with the provision of merit goods also need further elaboration. In chapter three we defend the provision of merit goods and point to three specific features of merit good provision. Merit goods interfere with consumer preferences and thus need a moral justification. Merit goods violate that principle that the consumer must pay for his consumption goods. Hence, a special method of financing merit goods must be proposed. In chapter four we ask the question as to how many domains there are where the government has to make merit good decisions. We develop arguments for eleven domains.

In reviewing the interpretation of the financial crisis of 2007–2008 and the ensuing recession we point out that Reinhart, Rogoff, Reich, and Rajan jointly make use of seven of my eleven categories of merit goods to explain that crisis and the ensuing recession. I present my arguments in chapter four.

In the analysis of the causes of the financial crisis of 2007–2008 an important role is assigned to deregulation and lack of government oversight and regulation of the banking system. Alan Greenspan, chair of the Federal Reserve from August 11, 1987—January 31, 2006, played an important role in decisions on whether or not to regulate and actively supervise the banking system prior to the crisis.

As reported by William Black in his essay on "The continuing saga of bank self-regulation and other fairy tales featuring Alan Greenspan" we learn that Greenspan

> supported the repeal of the Glass–Steagall Act despite the conflict of interest inherent in combining commercial and investment banking. He supported the passage of the Commodities Futures Modernization Act of 2000 despite agency conflicts between managers and owners of firms purchasing and selling credit default swaps (CDS).

> He opposed using the Fed's unique statutory authority under HOEPA (1994) to regulate ban fraudulent liar's loans by entities not regulated by the Federal government. He opposed efforts to clean up outside auditors' conflict of interest in serving as auditor and consultant to clients. He opposed efforts to clean up the acute agency conflicts of interest caused by modern executive compensation. He opposed taking an effective response to the large banks acting on their perverse conflicts of interest to aid and abet Enron's SPV frauds.

In his testimony to the House Committee on Oversight and Government Reform Greenspan said: "Those of us who have looked to the self-interest of lending institutions to protect shareholders' equity, myself included, are in a state of shocked disbelief" (Andrews in New York Times, October 23, 2008).

In Greenspan's talk to Wharton we find Greenspan providing the philosophical argument on why Greenspan sees a connection between self-interest and lack of urgency for regulating the banking sector.

Greenspan first introduces the fact that in many transactions trust in the other, even trust in the word of the other is a normal fact of business life. He said:

> The principles governing business behavior are an essential support to voluntary exchange, the defining characteristic of free markets. Voluntary exchange, in turn, **implies trust in the word** of those with whom we do business. To be sure, all market economies

require a rule of law to function–laws of contracts, rights to property, and a general protection of citizens from arbitrary actions of the state. Yet, if even a small fraction of legally binding transactions required adjudication, our court systems would be swamped into immobility, and a rule of law would be unenforceable [My emphasis].

Greenspan next makes of trust in others a necessary condition of the current economic scene. He says:

Of necessity, therefore, in virtually all our transactions, whether with customers or with colleagues, with friends or with strangers, **we rely on the word of those with whom we do business**. If we could not do so, goods and services could not be exchanged efficiently [My emphasis].

Greenspan then points out that trust is unavoidable and thus useful. He says:

Trillions of dollars of assets are priced and traded daily in our financial markets. Before recent technologies enabled transactions to clear and settle virtually in real time, most of the vast volumes of trades were not legally binding for days. **Their validity rested on trust**. Even today, much of business is transacted on parties' undocumented verbal agreements [My emphasis].

Moreover, even when followed to the letter, laws guide only a few of the day-to-day decisions required of business and financial managers. The rest are governed by whatever personal code of values market participants bring to the table.

Greenspan next develops the argument that free competition gave a premium on trust and punished violation with the example of driving untrustworthy economic agents out business. He relies for his argument on freewheeling nineteenth-century America:

Trust as the necessary condition for commerce was particularly evident in freewheeling nineteenth-century America, where reputation became a valued asset. Throughout much of that century, laissez-faire reigned in the United States as elsewhere, and caveat emptor was the prevailing prescription for guarding against wide-open trading practices. In such an environment, **a reputation for honest dealing**, which many feared was in short supply, **was particularly valued**. Even those inclined to be less than scrupulous in their personal dealings **had to adhere to a more ethical standard** in their market transactions, or they **risked being driven out of business** [My emphasis].

Finally, Greenspan concedes that there are examples of businesses which violated that trust. But he argues that they are a distinct minority. Furthermore he claims that the success of American free market economy could not have been so great if corporate America had been seriously flawed. He said it this way:

To be sure, the history of world business, then and now, is strewn with Fisks, Goulds, Ponzis and numerous others treading on, or over, the edge of legality. But, despite their prominence, **they were a distinct minority**. If the situation had been otherwise, late nineteenth- and early twentieth-century America would never have realized so high a standard of living. Indeed, we could not have achieved our current level of national productivity if ethical behavior had not been the norm or if corporate governance had been deeply flawed [My emphasis].

In my reading of Adam Smith in chapter one, I find a form of reasoning which contradicts the reasoning of Greenspan. And it is a form of reasoning that applies to the question of the need for banking regulation. Adam Smith observed the current practices of his time. He saw that people could accept money in any amount from anybody and simply give in return an I-owe-you-note. But the "I-owe-you-note" giver could be a "beggarly banker." This could create many calamities, so argues Smith. Hence, he proposes regulation of the banking sector. He defends the limitation of freedom by the merit good idea that the good of the whole society justifies the limitation of individual freedom. Here is his argument:

> But those exertions of the natural liberty of a few individuals, which might endanger the security of the whole society, are, and ought to be, restrained by the laws of all governments, of the most free as well as of the most despotical. The obligation of building party walls, in order to prevent the communication of fire, is a violation of natural liberty exactly of the same kind with the regulations of the banking trade which are here proposed (Smith, 308).

Adam Smith thus presents us both with a defense of the free competitive market and with arguments for a crucial role for the government in dealing with public and merit goods. Adam Smith himself argues that the government has a compelling regulatory function with reference to the banking system. In formulating his argument he uses the logic of the merit good argumentation as first articulated explicitly in contemporary economic theory by Musgrave. In chapter four of this book we show that Reinhart, Rogoff, Reich, and Rajan build their analyses of the financial crisis of 2007–2008 and the ensuing recession on seven of the eleven merit good categories I argue for in chapter three. I hope that this book on philosophy of economics can help seeing clearer the complexities of our contemporary free market economy. I hope to contribute by this book to the idea that our free market economy needs much intelligent regulation.

References

Andrews EL (2008) Greenspan concedes error on regulation. http://www.nytimes.com/2008/10/24/business/economy/24panel.html?_r=1&ref=edmundlandrews. New York Times, 23 Oct 2008, p B1
Black W (2012) Greenspan's Laissez Fairy tale. http://neweconomicperspectives.org/2012/01/greenspans-laissez-fairy-tale.html and http://www.benzinga.com/general/politics/12/01/2248082/greenspans-laissez-fairy-tale (Kansas-City, MO)
Greenspan A (2005) Commencement address. Wharton School, University of Pennsylvania, Philadelphia. http://www.federalreserve.gov/boarddocs/speeches/2005/20050515/
Smith A (1937) The wealth of nations. The Modern Library, New York

Chapter 2
Adam Smith and the Free Market

Abstract In this chapter I show Adam Smith's great admiration for the new free market economy that is exemplified by his report on the enormous productivity of the pin-factory. Smith attributes this great productivity to the division of labor which allows workers to specialize and which encourages them, out of self-interest, to look for machines to help in their work. On the demand side, the new economy relies on the human tendency to barter where self-interest replaces friendship as the means to get what one wants. This tendency to barter entices the system to produce what people want at the cheapest possible price. This is, according to Smith, the presence of a kind of "invisible hand." It is not the result of a (government) plan. Next, I show that Smith, provides an argument that the help of the government is needed in the case of the provision of roads thereby prefiguring the modern concept of public goods. I show how Smith anticipates the modern concept of merit good in his discussion of education, monopolies and the need of governmental control of banking. Smith even discusses the danger of lobbying to influence the regulatory power of the state.

Keywords Adam Smith • The new economy • Self-interest • Tendency to barter • Invisible hand • Public goods • Merit goods • Function of the government • Banking regulations • Lobbying

2.1 Introduction

In preparation for our reflections on the financial crisis of 2007–2008 and the subsequent recession, I would like to highlight some of the most important insights that Adam Smith has given us about the new emerging economy of his time, now referred to as the free market economy or capitalism. Adam Smith's text, of course, provides elegantly formulated arguments for a free market liberated from undue interference by the government.

Adam Smith's text, however, also gives convincing arguments for a humble helping function for the government. Thus, where individuals are not motivated by their self-interest to pay for a service which is beneficial for the whole society,

W. Ver Eecke, *Ethical Reflections on the Financial Crisis 2007/2008*, SpringerBriefs in Economics, DOI: 10.1007/978-3-642-35091-7_2,
© The Author(s) 2013

then, so argues Smith, the government should help. But the government should provide the help in such a way that the ones who benefit directly from the service and benefit the most are forced to pay relatively the most. Modern economic theory has developed this insight into the technical problem of the efficient and just provision of public goods: i.e., goods which many can enjoy without the enjoyment of another consumer diminishing the enjoyment of the first but where the enjoyment is possible as soon as one consumer has bought the service without the possibility of excluding the non-paying consumer. These two curious characteristics of some economic goods are, in contemporary economic theory, referred to as being non-rival in consumption and being non-excludable. Adam Smith already saw that public goods could be provided in such a way that the self-interest of all consumers was respected, even if the help of the government might be necessary to provide the service.

Adam Smith also argues that in some cases the government can, on moral grounds, overrule the self-interest of consumers. Thus, he advocates the idea that the government should provide help for the education of the poor because that is the right thing to do. Clearly, in such a case, the principle that the benefitting consumer should pay does not apply. Adam Smith then provides a new method of paying: i.e., ability to pay. Centuries later, Richard Musgrave created a name for such goods and called them merit goods. Indeed, Musgrave defined merit goods as goods that are so meritorious that there are morally legitimate reasons for interference with consumer sovereignty. When Adam Smith advocates the idea that banking should be regulated in order to safeguard the banking system we see in that argument another clear example of Musgrave's concept of merit good (Smith, 308 and 313).

The opposite of merit goods are called demerit goods. Demerit goods are goods which have such detrimental effects that there are moral reasons for interfering with consumer sovereignty in order to diminish the level of consumption of such goods. Many problems have been raised in the economic literature about the validity (McLure; Wildavsky) and the applicability (Mackscheidt; Head; Folkers; Brennan & Lomasky) of this new concept. In a subsequent chapter I argue that there are eleven domains where the government has moral grounds to impose a regulatory function on the free market. I will also show how Rajan uses seven of these categories to explain the financial crisis of 2007–2008 and the subsequent recession. Let us, however, return to Adam Smith.

2.2 Adam Smith's Admiration for the Productivity of the New Economy

Adam Smith was overwhelmingly impressed by the new free market economy of his time. This impression was the incident that caused him to think about the principles that made the new economy so successful. As I want to make use of Adam Smith to develop the principles that we should be using in order to analyze our contemporary economy, I want to quote Adam Smith rather than paraphrase him.

Adam Smith exemplified the enormous success of the new economy by means of the example of the pin factory. Here is his enthusiastic description of his observation:

> To take an example, therefore, from a very trifling manufacture; but one in which the division of labour has been very often taken notice of, the trade of the pin-maker; a workman not educated to this business (which the division of labour has rendered a distinct trade), nor acquainted with the use of the machinery employed in it (to the invention of which the same division of labour has probably given occasion), could scarce, perhaps, with his utmost industry, make one pin in a day, and certainly could not make twenty. But in the way in which this business is now carried on, not only the whole work is a peculiar trade, but it is divided into a number of branches, of which the greater part are likewise peculiar trades. One man draws out the wire, another straights it, a third cuts it, a fourth points it, a fifth grinds it at the top for receiving the head; to make the head requires two or three distinct operations; to put it on, is a peculiar business, to whiten the pins is another; it is even a trade by itself to put them into the paper; and the important business of making a pin is, in this manner, divided into about eighteen distinct operations, which, in some manufactories, are all performed by distinct hands, though in others the same man will sometimes perform two or three of them. I have seen a small manufactory of this kind where ten men only were employed, and where some of them consequently performed two or three distinct operations. But though they were very poor, and therefore but indifferently accommodated with the necessary machinery, they could, when they exerted themselves, make among them about twelve pounds of pins in a day. There are in a pound upwards of four thousand pins of a middling size. Those ten persons, therefore, could make among them upwards of forty-eight thousand pins in a day. Each person, therefore, making a tenth part of forty-eight thousand pins, might be considered as making four thousand eight hundred pins in a day. But if they had all wrought separately and independently, and without any of them having been educated to this peculiar business, they certainly could not each of them have made twenty, perhaps not one pin in a day; that is, certainly, not the two hundred and fortieth, perhaps not the four thousand eight hundredth part of what they are at present capable of performing, in consequence of a proper division and combination of their different operations (4–5).

2.3 Adam Smith on the Production Side of the New Economy

Adam Smith's first conclusion concentrates upon the production side of the new economy. He will later pay attention to the demand side of the economy.

Adam Smith stresses the fact that the new economy has miraculous productivity and he connects that productivity with the division of labor. He observes that: "The division of labour, however, so far as it can be introduced, occasions, in every art, a proportionable increase of the productive powers of labour"(5). Adam Smith then argues that:

> This great increase of the quantity of work which, in consequence of the division of labour, the same number of people are capable of performing, is owing to three different circumstances; first to the increase of dexterity in every particular workman; secondly, to the saving of the time which is commonly lost in passing from one species of work to another; and lastly, to the invention of a great number of machines which facilitate and abridge labour, and enable one man to do the work of many (5).

Adam Smith pays special attention to the third point. For the first time, he here connects the idea of economic productivity with the miraculous incentive created by self-interest. He does so by the plausible, but probably mythical, story of the boy who wanted more play time and invented an improvement of the engine not for the greater profitability of the factory where he worked but for his own self-interest in more playtime. This is a humble introduction of an idea which he later will make a general principle when writing: "he intends only his own gain, and he is in this, as in many other case, led by an invisible hand to produce an end which was no part of his intention" (423).

About the connection between self-interest and the invention of better or new machines he writes:

> I shall only observe, therefore, that the invention of all those machines by which labour is so much facilitated and abridged, seems to have been originally owing to the division of labour. Men are much more likely to discover easier and readier methods of attaining any object, when the whole attention of their minds is directed towards that single object, than when it is dissipated among a great variety of things. But in consequence of the division of labour, the whole of every man's attention comes naturally to be directed towards some one very simple object. It is naturally to be expected, therefore, that some one or other of those who are employed in each particular branch of labour should soon find out easier and readier methods of performing their own particular work, wherever the nature of it admits of such improvement. A great part of the machines made use of in those manufactures in which labour is most subdivided, were originally the inventions of common workmen, who, being each of them employed in some very simple operation, naturally turned their thoughts towards finding out easier and readier methods of performing it. Whoever has been much accustomed to visit such manufactures, must frequently have been shewn very pretty machines, which were the inventions of such workmen, in order to facilitate and quicken their own particular part of the work. In the first fire-engines, a boy was constantly employed to open and shut alternately the communication between the boiler and the cylinder, according as the piston either ascended or descended. One of those boys, who loved to play with his companions, observed that, by tying a string from the handle of the valve which opened this communication, to another part of the machine, the valve would open and shut without his assistance, and leave him at liberty to divert himself with his play-fellows. One of the greatest improvements that has been made upon this machine, since it was first invented, was in this manner the discovery of a boy who wanted to save his own labour (9).

While meditating about the great productivity of the new economy Adam Smith makes an economic, a sociological and a world historical observation. The economic observation made by Smith is that this division of labor multiplies the need for exchange. Thus he writes:

> It is the great multiplication of the productions of all the different arts, in consequence of the division of labour, which occasions, in a well-governed society, that universal opulence which extends itself to the lowest ranks of the people. Every workman has a great quantity of his own work to dispose of beyond what he himself has occasion for; and every other workman being exactly in the same situation, he is enabled to exchange a great quantity of his own goods for a great quantity, or, what comes to the same thing, for the price of a great quantity of theirs (11).

The sociological observation Smith makes is that everybody in a society with the new economy is better off, and presumably necessarily so. This crucial observation and/or conclusion will appear again later and is important to keep in mind. Adam Smith writes:

> He [every workman] supplies them [every other workman] abundantly with what they have occasion for, and they accommodate him as amply with what he has occasion for, and a general plenty diffuses itself through all the different ranks of the society (11).

The world historical observation, even if done in a discriminatory tone not acceptable today, is that in the new economy a frugal peasant is better off than an African king. Here is how Smith says it:

> Compared, indeed, with the more extravagant luxury of the great, his accommodation must no doubt appear extremely simple and easy; and yet it may be true, perhaps, that the accommodation of an European prince does not always so much exceed that of an industrious and frugal peasant, as the accommodation of the latter exceeds that of many an African king, the absolute master of the lives and liberties of ten thousand naked savages (12).

Before reflecting on the demand side of the new economy, Adam Smith again anticipates the principle of the "invisible hand." He writes: "This division of labour, from which so many advantages are derived, is not originally the effect of any human wisdom, which foresees and intends that general opulence to which it gives occasion" (13).

2.4 Adam Smith and the Demand Side of the New Economy

Adam Smith next turns to the demand side of the new economy. He points to the idea of bartering within the context of a contractual exchange as central for thinking about the demand side of the new economy. He writes that the new economy is not the result of human wisdom or planning but rather results from "the propensity to truck, barter, and exchange one thing for another" (13). He then further specifies that this tendency to barter

> is common to all men, and to be found in no other race of animals, which seem to know neither this nor any other species of contracts. Two greyhounds, in running down the same hare, have sometimes the appearance of acting in some sort of concert. Each turns her towards his companion, or endeavours to intercept her when his companion turns her towards himself. This, however, is not the effect of any contract, but of the accidental concurrence of their passions in the same object at that particular time. Nobody ever saw a dog make a fair and deliberate exchange of one bone for another with another dog. Nobody ever saw one animal by its gestures and natural cries signify to another, this is mine, that yours; I am willing to give this for that (13).

Adam Smith makes some additional observations upon the role of bartering in the new economy; first, he points out that without the tendency or the willingness to barter, the productive miracle of the new economy would not make sense. He writes:

> without the disposition to truck, barter, and exchange, every man must have procured to himself every necessary and conveniency of life which he wanted. All must have

had the same duties to perform, and the same work to do, and there could have been no such difference of employment as could alone give occasion to any great difference of talents (16).

But with the tendency to barter, everybody can make use of the skills and productivity of everybody else. Adam Smith says it this way:

> the most dissimilar geniuses are of use to one another; the different produces of their respective talents, by the general disposition to truck, barter, and exchange, being brought, as it were, into a common stock, where every man may purchase whatever part of the produce of other men's talents he has occasion for (16).

Second, Smith in two steps introduces the idea that the new economy requires a new social ethic. That new ethic cannot be based on the Christian idea of love and friendship but must be based on that non-Christian idea of self-interest. The inability to use friendship as the basis of the motivation for the new economy is demonstrated by a simple common sense observation. Smith writes:

> In civilized society he stands at all times in need of the cooperation and assistance of great multitudes, while his whole life is scarce sufficient to gain the friendship of a few persons. In almost every other race of animals each individual, when it is grown up to maturity, is entirely independent, and in its natural state has occasion for the assistance of no other living creature. But man has almost constant occasion for the help of his brethren, and it is in vain for him to expect it from their benevolence only (14).

Having shown that the new economy cannot depend on friendship, love or benevolence, Adam Smith reintroduces as basic motive on the demand side of the economy the same motive he found to be so central on the production side: self-interest. He says it this way:

> Whoever offers to another a bargain of any kind, proposes to do this. Give me that which I want, and you shall have this which you want, is the meaning of every such offer; and it is in this manner that we obtain from one another the far greater part of those good offices which we stand in need of. It is not from the benevolence of the butcher, the brewer, or the baker, that we expect our dinner, but from their regard to their own interest. We address ourselves, not to their humanity but to their self-love, and never talk to them of our own necessities but of their advantages. Nobody but a beggar chuses to depend chiefly upon the benevolence of his fellow-citizens (14).

Adam Smith thus corrects Hobbes. Both agree that human beings can be and, de facto unavoidably are, competitors if not enemies. However, Adam Smith sees that the tendency to barter within an environment of socially protected contracts avoids the need for deadly Hobbesian competition and replaces it with the co-operative competition of the new economy.

Adam Smith then reflects on what could be an obstacle for the indefinite expansion of the benefits of the new economy. He asks the simple question as to what people will do with the ever increasing amount of goods that this new productive economy is producing. Adam Smith says it this way:

> As it is the power of exchanging that gives occasion to the division of labour, so the extent of this division must always be limited by the extent of that power, or, in other words, by the extent of the market. When the market is very small, no person can have any encouragement to dedicate himself entirely to one employment, for want of the power to exchange

all that surplus part of the produce of his own labour, which is over and above his own consumption, for such parts of the produce of other men's labour as he has occasion for (17).

Adam Smith then links the extent of the market to the availability of cheap transportation which allows for more people to exchange products without the cost of transportation thus making the products excessively expensive. He then points out that waterways have often been the natural way of providing cheap transportation. In a beautiful summary Smith states:

> In Bengal the Ganges and several other great rivers form a great number of navigable canals in the same manner as the Nile does in Egypt. In the Eastern provinces of China too, several great rivers form, by their different branches, a multitude of canals, and by communicating with one another afford an inland navigation much more extensive than that either of the Nile or the Ganges, or perhaps than both of them put together. It is remarkable that neither the ancient Egyptians, nor the Indians, nor the Chinese, encouraged foreign commerce, but seem all to have derived their great opulence from this inland navigation.

> All the inland parts of Africa, and all that part of Asia which lies any considerable way north of the Euxine and Caspian seas, the ancient Scythia, the modern Tartary and Siberia, seem in all ages of the world to have been in the same barbarous and uncivilized state in which we find them at present. The sea of Tartary is the frozen ocean which admits of no navigation, and though some of the greatest rivers in the world run through that country, they are at too great a distance from one another to carry commerce and communication through the greater part of it. There are in Africa none of those great inlets, such as the Baltic and Adriatic seas in Europe, the Mediterranean and Euxine seas in both Europe and Asia, and the gulps of Arabia, Persia, India, Bengal, and Siam, in Asia, to carry maritime commerce into the interior parts of that great continent: and the great rivers of Africa are at too great a distance from one another to give occasion to any considerable inland navigation (20–21).

The limited availability of transportation by water naturally poses the question of other means of transportation. This will allow Adam Smith to give the government a modest and limited role in the new economy. The government should play a role in the provision of infrastructure needed for the new economy, particularly roads.

2.5 Adam Smith's General Principles for a Productive Economy

While making astute observations about the new productive economy, Adam Smith inductively introduces general principles which can explain the productivity of the new economy. These general principles will then become normative for the idea of the free market. A first such general principle is the idea that government intervention in the economy is mostly counterproductive. Smith comes to such a conclusion in two steps. First, he analyzes the economic effects of the human tendency to barter and, simultaneously, to keep their self-interest in mind. Second, he studies the historical periods where the government managed the economy by either mercantilist or physiocratic principles.

When analyzing the human tendency to barter, Adam Smith argues that human beings will offer to pay more for goods they want and that are in short supply. He also argues that producers will be forced to accept a lower price for goods that are overproduced in order to be able to sell them. Smith thus argues that self-interest in exchange will entice everybody to produce most efficiently what everybody wants. This is how Smith says it:

> The market price of every particular commodity is regulated by the proportion between the quantity which is actually brought to market, and the demand of those who are willing to pay the natural price of the commodity, or the whole value of the rent, labour, and profit, which must be paid in order to bring it thither. Such people may be called the effectual demanders, and their demand the effectual demand; since it may be sufficient to effectuate the bringing of the commodity to market. It is different from the absolute demand. A very poor man may be said in some sense to have a demand for a coach and six; he might like to have it; but his demand is not an effectual demand, as the commodity can never be brought to market in order to satisfy it.

> When the quantity of any commodity which is brought to market falls short of the effectual demand, all those who are willing to pay the whole value of the rent, wages, and profit, which must be paid in order to bring it thither, cannot be supplied with the quantity which they want. Rather than want it altogether, some of them will be willing to give more. A competition will immediately begin among them, and the market price will rise more or less above the natural price, according as either the greatness of the deficiency, or the wealth and wanton luxury of the competitors, happen to animate more or less the eagerness of the competition. Among competitors of equal wealth and luxury the same deficiency will generally occasion a more or less eager competition, according as the acquisition of the commodity happens to be of more or less importance to them. Hence the exorbitant price of the necessaries of life during the blockade of a town or in a famine (56).

Adam Smith then develops the second part of his argument for limited government when he analyzes the different systems of political economy which preceded the new economy in book five of *The Wealth of Nations*: the Mercantile system and what Smith calls the Agricultural system or what is known nowadays as the Physiocratic system. After having demonstrated the deficiencies of these two government policies which justified the intervention in economics, Adam Smith generalizes his own conclusion as follows:

> It is thus that every system which endeavours, either by extraordinary encouragements to draw towards a particular species of industry a greater share of the capital of the society than what would naturally go to it, or, by extraordinary restraints, force from a particular species of industry some share of the capital which would otherwise be employed in it, is in reality subversive of the great purpose which it means to promote. It retards, instead of accelerating, the progress of the society towards real wealth and greatness; and diminishes, instead of increasing, the real value of the annual produce of its land and labour (650–651).

The above analysis invites Smith then to give a laudatory statement for the new economic system of full free enterprise. He says it eloquently as follows:

> All systems either of preference or of restraint, therefore, being thus completely taken away, the obvious and simple system of natural liberty establishes itself of its own accord. Every man, as long as he does not violate the laws of justice, is left perfectly free to pursue his own interest his own way, and to bring both his industry and capital into competition with those of any other man, or order of men. The sovereign is completely discharged from a duty, in the attempting to perform which he must always be exposed to innumerable delusions, and for the proper performance of which no human wisdom or knowledge could ever be sufficient; the duty of superintending the industry of private people, and of directing it towards the employments most suitable to the interest of the society (651).

Let us notice some strong conclusions. First, Adam Smith forcefully argues that the government has generally no constructive role to play in the new miraculously efficient economy based on division of labor and self-interested bartering. If the government has nevertheless a possible function it will have to be argued for sharply. We will provide later Smith's arguments for two categories of justified government roles: i.e., proper provision of public goods and interference for the provision of merit goods. Second, Smith makes the assumption that once the government stops meddling with the economy then "the obvious and simple system [of natural liberty of the new free market economy] establishes itself of its own accord" (651). Third, Adam Smith puts one explicit limit to the pursuit of self-interest namely the "laws of justice" (651). And where the neo-liberals will show that cartels and trusts are a permanent danger to the new economy, there Smith softly suggests that monopolies might be regulated. Thus he writes: "upon the expiration of the term [of a patent], the monopoly ought to determine ["to determine" means "to end"]" (712). Smith goes on to say:

> By a perpetual monopoly, all the other subjects of the state are taxed very absurdly in two different ways; first, by the high price of goods, which, in the case of free trade, they could buy much cheaper; and, secondly, by their total exclusion from a branch of business, which it might be both convenient and profitable for many of them to carry on (Ibid).

He then makes the proposal that "where there is an exclusive corporation, it may perhaps be proper to regulate the price of the first necessary of life [i.e., bread]" (142). But Smith immediate expresses his opinion that a free competitive market will do better. Thus he writes: "But where there is none [i.e., an exclusive corporation], the competition will regulate it much better than any assize." (Ibid).

2.6 Adam Smith About Some Necessary Functions for the Government

We should notice that Adam Smith amends his laudatory statement for the new free market economy with a simple caviat. There are things the government has to do. Smith enumerates three functions for the government: defense against foreign invasions; guaranteeing justice for one's own citizens; and the provision of public works. All three of which are more likely the wealthier a nation is. This is how Smith formulates it:

> According to the system of natural liberty, the sovereign has only three duties to attend to; three duties of great importance, indeed, but plain and intelligible to common understandings: first, the duty of protecting the society from violence and invasion of other independent societies; secondly, the duty of protecting, as far as possible, every member of the society from the injustice or oppression of every other member of it, or the duty of establishing an exact administration of justice; and, thirdly, the duty of erecting and maintaining certain public works and certain public institutions which it can never be for the

interest of any individual, or small number of individuals, to erect and maintain; because the profit could never repay the expense to any individual or small number of individuals, though it may frequently do much more than repay it to a great society (651).

When Adam Smith discusses the method of payment for government services he gives a slightly larger series of government functions. Here is that larger list of government functions:

The expense of defending the society, and that of supporting the dignity of the chief magistrate, are both laid out for the general benefit of the whole society. It is reasonable, therefore, that they should be defrayed by the general contribution of the whole society, all the different members contributing, as nearly as possible, in proportion to their respective abilities.

The expense of the administration of justice, too, may, no doubt, be considered as laid out for the benefit of the whole society. There is no impropriety, therefore, in its being defrayed by the general contribution of the whole society. The persons, however, who gave occasion to this expense are those who, by their injustice in one way or another, make it necessary to seek redress or protection from the courts of justice. The persons again most immediately benefited by this expense are those whom the courts of justice either restore to their rights or maintain in their rights. The expense of the administration of justice, therefore, may very properly be defrayed by the particular contribution of one or other, or both, of those two different sets of persons, according as different occasions may require, that is, by the fees of court. It cannot be necessary to have recourse to the general contribution of the whole society, except for the conviction of those criminals who have not themselves any estate or fund sufficient for paying those fees.

Those local or provincial expenses of which the benefit is local or provincial (what is laid out, for example, upon the police of a particular town or district) ought to be defrayed by a local or provincial revenue, and ought to be no burden upon the general revenue of the society. It is unjust that the whole society should contribute towards an expense of which the benefit is confined to a part of the society.

The expense of maintaining good roads and communications is, no doubt, beneficial to the whole society, and may, therefore, without any injustice. be defrayed by the general contribution of the whole society. This expense, however, is most immediately and directly beneficial to those who travel or carry goods from one place to another, and to those who consume such goods. The turnpike tolls in England, and the duties called peages in other countries, lay it altogether upon those two different sets of people, and thereby discharge the general revenue of the society from a very considerable burden.

The expense of the institutions for education and religious instruction is likewise, no doubt, beneficial to the whole society, and may, therefore, without injustice, be defrayed by the general contribution of the whole society. This expense, however, might perhaps with equal propriety, and even with some advantage, be defrayed altogether by those who receive the immediate benefit of such education and instruction, or by the voluntary contribution of those who think they have occasion for either the one or the other.

When the institutions or public works which are beneficial to the whole society either cannot be maintained altogether, or are not maintained altogether by the contribution of such particular members of the society as are most immediately benefited by them, the deficiency must in most cases be made up by the general contribution of the whole society. The general revenue of the society, over and above defraying the expense of defending the society, and of supporting the dignity of the chief magistrate, must make up for the deficiency of many particular branches of revenue (767–768).

Besides adding the duty to support the chief magistrate, Adam Smith also adds the duty of providing education and religious instruction. In this latter quotation we find that Adam Smith introduces two different principles for financing the many functions of the government: the first principle is described for defending the society and for the financing of the "dignity of the chief magistrate" and also applies, at least partially, for the administration of justice and education. Here is Smith's articulation of that principle for paying for the costs of these government services: they are "laid out for the general benefit of the whole society," (767) hence "they should be defrayed by the general contribution of the whole society, all the different members contributing, as nearly as possible, in proportion to their respective abilities" (767). The second principle which applies for maintaining good roads and communication is described as follows:

> This expense, however, is most immediately and directly beneficial to those who travel or carry goods from one place to another, and to those who consume such goods. The turnpike tolls in England, and the duties called peages in other countries, lay it altogether upon those two different sets of people, and thereby discharge the general revenue of the society from a very considerable burden (767).

The second principle is what is now called the principle of financing "public goods." According to that principle individuals should pay according to their benefit of the service. Such financing has its technical difficulties, but obeys where possible Smith's principle of bartering: "Do ut des." The first principle is a totally different method of paying for government services. It does not connect one's utility of the service to the amount one is charged. Instead one is charged according to ability to pay. In this case the much praised principle of self-interest cannot be called upon to justify the imposition of payments. Instead Smith appeals to another principle: the payment is laid out for a service which is to "the general benefit of the whole society" (767). Adam Smith provides specific justifications for defense and education. Adam Smith presents the argument that in the case of training for defense or in giving education, the government is providing a good worthy of itself. Adam Smith explicitly excludes the utility calculus for these goods. Thus about cowardice which is countered by training for defense, Adam Smith writes the following:

> But a coward, a man incapable either of defending or of revenging himself, evidently wants one of the most essential parts of the character of a man. He is as much mutilated and deformed in his mind as another is in his body, who is either deprived of some of its most essential members, or has lost the use of them. He is evidently the more wretched and miserable of the two; because happiness and misery, which reside altogether in the mind, must necessarily depend more upon the healthful or unhealthful, the mutilated or entire state of the mind, than upon that of the body. Even though the martial spirit of the people were of no use towards the defence of the society, yet to prevent that sort of mental mutilation, deformity, and wretchedness, which cowardice necessarily involves in it, from spreading themselves through the great body of the people, would still deserve the most serious attention of government, in the same manner as it would deserve its most serious attention to prevent a leprosy or any other loathsome and offensive disease, though neither mortal nor dangerous, from spreading itself among them, though perhaps no other public good might result from such attention besides the prevention of so great a public evil (739).

And about the need for education, Adam Smith has this to say:

The same thing may be said of the gross ignorance and stupidity which, in a civilized society, seem so frequently to benumb the understandings of all the inferior ranks of people. A man without the proper use of the intellectual faculties of a man, is, if possible, more contemptible than even a coward, and seems to be mutilated and deformed in a still more essential part of the character of human nature. Though the state was to derive no advantage from the instruction of the inferior ranks of people, it would still deserve its attention that they should not be altogether uninstructed (739–740).[1]

We feel that this group of services neatly fits the category of goods described by Musgrave as "merit' or "demerit" goods. They have moral value and do not respect the self-interest principle in the financing method. Adam Smith in several specific cases of what we like to call merit good provisions explicitly mentions either the limitations of self-interest or the limitations of freedom in describing the provision of such services. Thus about education and training for defense he writes:

The public can impose upon almost the whole body of the people the necessity of acquiring those most essential parts of education, by obliging every man to undergo an examination or probation in them before he can obtain the freedom in any corporation, or be allowed to set up any trade either in a village or town corporate.

It was in this manner, by facilitating the acquisition of their military and gymnastic exercises, by encouraging it, and even by imposing upon the whole body of the people the necessity of learning those exercises, that the Greek and Roman republics maintained the martial spirit of their respective citizens" (738).

Adam Smith makes a similar argument about property rights. He writes:

The acquisition of valuable and extensive property, therefore, necessarily requires the establishment of civil government. Where there is no property, or at least none that exceeds the value of 2 or 3 days labour, civil government is not so necessary.

Civil government supposes a certain subordination. But as the necessity of civil government gradually grows up with the acquisition of valuable property, so the principal causes which naturally introduce subordination gradually grow up with the growth of that valuable property (670).

Or even more sharply: "Civil government, so far as it is instituted for the security of property, is in reality instituted for the defence of the rich against the poor, or of those who have some property against those who have none at all" (674).

It is worth noting, in light of the financial crisis of 2007–2008, that Adam Smith himself advocates also certain limitations on the banks. Thus he writes:

Where the issuing of bank notes for such very small sums is allowed and commonly practised, many mean people are both enabled and encouraged to become bankers. A person

---

[1] James Stanfield wrote a brief and perceptive article on several aspects of Smith's views on education. See: http://research.ncl.ac.uk/egwest/articles/ieaarticles/Adam_Smith_on_Education.pdf

whose promissory note for five pounds, or even for twenty shillings, would be rejected by everybody, will get it to be received without scruple when it is issued for so small a sum as a sixpence. But the frequent bankruptcies to which such beggarly bankers must be liable may occasion a very considerable inconveniency, and sometimes even a very great calamity to many poor people who had received their notes in payment.

It were better, perhaps, that no bank notes were issued in any part of the kingdom for a smaller sum than five pounds. Paper money would then, probably, confine itself, in every part of the kingdom, to the circulation between the different dealers, as much as it does at present in London, where no bank notes are issued under ten pounds value; five pounds being, in most parts of the kingdom, a sum which, though it will purchase, little more than half the quantity of goods, is as much considered, and is as seldom spent all at once, as ten pounds are amidst the profuse expense of London (307).

Adam Smith explicitly acknowledges that these restraints are a limitation on freedom, but he justifies them in the name of the good of the banking system as a whole. Here is how he explains his worry and simultaneously his defense for banking regulations:

To restrain private people, it may be said, from receiving in payment the promissory notes of a banker, for any sum whether great or small, when they themselves are willing to receive them, or to restrain a banker from issuing such notes, when all his neighbours are willing to accept of them, is a manifest violation of that natural liberty which it is the proper business of law not to infringe, but to support. Such regulations may, no doubt, be considered as in some respects a violation of natural liberty. But those exertions of the natural liberty of a few individuals, which might endanger the security of the whole society, are, and ought to be, restrained by the laws of all governments, of the most free as well as of the most despotical. The obligation of building party walls, in order to prevent the communication of fire, is a violation of natural liberty exactly of the same kind with the regulations of the banking trade which are here proposed (308).

Adam Smith then almost boastingly reports what he sees as the great achievement of imposing this limited restraint on banking:

A paper money consisting in bank notes, issued by people of undoubted credit, payable upon demand without any condition, and in fact always readily paid as soon as presented, is, in every respect, equal in value to gold and silver money; since gold and silver money can at any time be had for it. Whatever is either bought or sold for such paper must necessarily be bought or sold as cheap as it could have been for gold and silver (308).

Adam Smith finishes his reflections on banking by putting his advocated restrictions on banking as a minor exception within the overall rule of free competition being the ideal for the new economy. He says it this way:

If bankers are restrained from issuing any circulating bank notes, or notes payable to the bearer, for less than a certain sum, and if they are subjected to the obligation of an immediate and unconditional payment of such bank notes as soon as presented, their trade may, with safety to the public, be rendered in all other respects perfectly free. The late multiplication of banking companies in both parts of the United Kingdom, an event by which many people have been much alarmed, instead of diminishing, increases the security of the public. It obliges all of them to be more circumspect in their conduct, and, by not extending their currency beyond its due proportion to their cash, to guard themselves against those malicious runs which the rival ship of so many competitors is always ready to bring upon them. It restrains the circulation of each particular company within a narrower circle, and reduces their circulating notes to a smaller number.

By dividing the whole circulation into a greater number of parts, the failure of any one company, an accident which, in the course of things, must sometimes happen, becomes of less consequence to the public. This free competition, too, obliges all bankers to be more liberal in their dealings with their customers, lest their rivals should carry them away. In general, if any branch of trade, or any division of labour, be advantageous to the public, the freer and more general the competition, it will always be the more so (313).

2.7 Adam Smith and Ethical Expectation of the New Economy

We also find in Adam Smith the idea that the raising of income for the working class must be considered a good thing for the whole society since the working class is the majority of the people and what is good for the majority [and does not hurt other people][2] cannot be bad for the society as a whole. Adam Smith thus puts forward a humanistic goal for the economy which is splendidly fulfilled by the new economy: improve the lives of everybody including the poor by a steady economic growth. Thus he writes:

> The common complaint that luxury extends itself even to the lowest ranks of the people, and that the labouring poor will not now be contented with the same food, clothing and lodging which satisfied them in former times, may convince us that it is not the money price of labour only, but its real recompense, which has augmented.

> Is this improvement in the circumstances of the lower ranks of the people to be regarded as an advantage or as an inconveniency to the society? The answer seems at first sight abundantly plain. Servants, labourers and workmen of different kinds, make up the far greater part of every great political society. But what improves the circumstances of the greater part can never be regarded as an inconveniency to the whole. No society can surely be flourishing and happy, of which the far greater part of the members are poor and miserable. It is but equity, besides, that they who feed, cloth and lodge the whole body of the people, should have such a share of the produce of their own labour as to be themselves tolerably well fed, clothed and lodged (78–79).

Adam Smith stresses the role of a growing economy for the well being of the poor when he writes:

> It deserves to be remarked, perhaps, that it is in the progressive state, while the society is advancing to the further acquisition, rather than when it has acquired its full complement of riches, that the condition of the labouring poor, of the great body of the people, seems to be the happiest and the most comfortable. It is hard in the stationary, and miserable in the declining state. The progressive state is in reality the cheerful and the hearty state to all the different orders of the society. The stationary is dull; the declining melancholy (81).

---

[2] This exception is not explicitly stated in Adam Smith. We need to add it to make the principle plausible. But I believe that Smith's line of thinking is compatible with the exception I included.

2.8 Adam Smith About Social Classes and Lobbying

Adam Smith was also aware that his society was not monolithic. He saw at least three different classes with different interests, that sometimes coincided with that of the whole society and sometimes not, and that these different groups were very different in the forcefulness and shrewdness by which they were putting forth their own interest even if it was against the well-being of the society as a whole. Here is what Smith wrote:

> The whole annual produce of the land and labour of every country, or what comes to the same thing, the whole price of that annual produce, naturally divides itself, it has already been observed, into three parts; the rent of land, the wages of labour, and the profits of stock; and constitutes a revenue to three different orders of people; to those who live by rent, to those who live by wages, and to those who live by profit. These are the three great, original and constituent orders of every civilized society, from whose revenue that of every other order is ultimately derived.

> The interest of the first of those three great orders, it appears from what has been just now said, is strictly and inseparably connected with the general interest of the society. Whatever either promotes or obstructs the one, necessarily promotes or obstructs the other. When the public deliberates concerning any regulation of commerce or police, the proprietors of land never can mislead it, with a view to promote the interest of their own particular order; at least, if they have any tolerable knowledge of that interest. They are, indeed, too often defective in this tolerable knowledge. They are the only one of the three orders whose revenue costs them neither labour nor care, but comes to them, as it were, of its own accord, and independent of any plan or project of their own. That indolence, which is the natural effect of the ease and security of their situation, renders them too often, not only ignorant, but incapable of that application of mind which is necessary in order to foresee and understand the consequences of any public regulation.

> The interest of the second order, that of those who live by wages, is as strictly connected with the interest of the society as that of the first. The wages of the labourer, it has already been shewn, are never so high as when the demand for labour is continually rising, or when the quantity employed is every year increasing considerably. When this real wealth of the society becomes stationary, his wages are soon reduced to what is barely enough to enable him to bring up a family, or to continue the race of labourers. When the society declines, they fall even below this. The order of proprietors may, perhaps, gain more by the prosperity of the society, than that of labourers: but there is no order that suffers so cruelly from its decline. But though the interest of the labourer is strictly connected with that of the society, he is incapable either of comprehending that interest, or of understanding its connection with his own. His condition leaves him no time to receive the necessary information, and his education and habits are commonly such as to render him unfit to judge even though he was fully informed. In the public deliberations, therefore, his voice is little heard and less regarded, except upon some particular occasions, when his clamour is animated, set on, and supported by his employers, not for his, but their own particular purposes.

> His employers constitute the third order, that of those who live by profit. It is the stock that is employed for the sake of profit, which puts into motion the greater part of the useful labour of every society. The plans and projects of the employers of stock regulate and direct all the most important operations of labour, and profit is the end proposed by all those plans and projects. But the rate of profit does not, like rent and wages, rise with the prosperity, and fall with the declension of the society. On the contrary, it is naturally low in rich, and high in poor countries, and it is always highest in the countries which

are going fastest to ruin. The interest of this third order, therefore, has not the same connection with the general interest of the society as that of the other two. Merchants and master manufacturers are, in this order, the two classes of people who commonly employ the largest capitals, and who by their wealth draw to themselves the greatest share of the public consideration. As during their whole lives they are engaged in plans and projects, they have frequently more acuteness of understanding than the greater part of country gentlemen. As their thoughts, however, are commonly exercised rather about the interest of their own particular branch of business, than about that of the society, their judgment, even when given with the greatest candour (which it has not been upon every occasion) is much more to be depended upon with regard to the former of those two objects, than with regard to the latter. Their superiority over the country gentleman is, not so much in their knowledge of the public interest, as in their having a better knowledge of their own interest than he has of his. It is by this superior knowledge of their own interest that they have frequently imposed upon his generosity, and persuaded him to give up both his own interest and that of the public, from a very simple but honest conviction, that their interest, and not his, was the interest of the public. The interest of the dealers, however, in any particular branch of trade or manufactures, is always in some respects different from, and even opposite to, that of the public. To widen the market and to narrow the competition, is always the interest of the dealers. To widen the market may frequently be agreeable enough to the interest of the public; but to narrow the competition must always be against it, and can serve only to enable the dealers, by raising their profits above what they naturally would be, to levy, for their own benefit, an absurd tax upon the rest of their fellow-citizens. The proposal of any new law or regulation of commerce which comes from this order, ought always to be listened to with great precaution, and ought never to be adopted till after having been long and carefully examined, not only with the most scrupulous, but with the most suspicious attention. It comes from an order of men, whose interest is never exactly the same with that of the public, who have generally an interest to deceive and even to oppress the public, and who accordingly have, upon many occasions, both deceived and oppressed it" (248–250).

Adam Smith thus warns against

The proposal of any new law or regulation of commerce which comes from this order (the employers), ought always to be listened to with great precaution, and ought never to be adopted till after having been long and carefully examined, not only with the most scrupulous, but with the most suspicious attention (250).

I think we can interpret this warning as a warning against all proposals to change—or even not properly adapt—governmental regulations of the economy. One needs to be specifically alert if the proposal comes from a group whose interest in the case is in conflict with that of the society as a whole. One needs to be super alert if it comes from a group with shrewd power to influence the government. Adam Smith identified deep knowledge of the economic situation as being an important element in the power to influence the government.

2.9 Conclusion

We have seen that Adam Smith greatly admired the productivity of the new economic order he observed. He considered the division of labor a crucial factor in the great productivity of the new economic order. This division of labor made human beings all more dependent upon each other. Human beings produced very efficiently what they specialized in, but they needed to find other human beings with whom to exchange what they had in abundance with what they lacked. On the production side, self-interest pushed human beings to be productive as they were the beneficiaries of their efficiency. On the consumption side, people could count on the self-interest of the producers to offer the products they wanted. Thus self-interest replaced friendship as the reliable motive for the new economy. Furthermore, the self-interest of both the consumers and the producers encouraged the production of what people wanted because of the latter's willingness to pay. Thus Adam Smith presents the free market as the system forced to be efficient on the basis of the self-interest motive of the economic actors.

Adam Smith then demonstrates the inefficiencies of economic systems in which the government systematically interferes in economic matters, like Mercantilism and the Physiocratic economic system. The main theme of Adam Smith in his *The Wealth of Nations* is thus that the free market is efficient without the government and that economic systems where the government is involved are inefficient.

However, Adam Smith also presents a second line of thought. Thus he argues that the miracle of productive efficiency of the new economy is limited by the extent of the market. Smith even states that "to widen the market may frequently be agreeable to the interest of the publick" (250). And the market can be increased by proper transportation. This allows Adam Smith to argue that the government can provide a helping role. He then sketches the beginnings of the modern economic theory of public goods provision.

Adam Smith also introduces the idea of merit goods: i.e., goods which are so good that the government can interfere with the preferences of consumers. For such goods Adam Smith provides moral arguments such as the argument for education and for military training in order to instill courage and avoid cowardice. He also proposes a different justification for the financing of merit goods than the one he proposed for public goods. And as part of a meritorious economy Adam Smith points to the expectation that the working class too should benefit from the increased productivity of the new economy.

Finally, Adam Smith warns against what we would now call lobbying efforts.

We believe that this balanced view of the free market economy can provide us the intellectual framework to understand some of the most sophisticated analyses of the financial crisis of 2007–2008 and the subsequent depression.

Reference

Smith A (1937) The wealth of nations. The Modern Library, New York

Chapter 3
The Concepts of Private, Public and Merit Goods

Abstract In this chapter I expand on Adam Smith's observation that roads and education cannot be conceptualized satisfactorily by the concept of private goods. The concepts of public and merit goods need to be added. I reduce the eighteen different characteristics of public goods, found in the economic literature, to the two crucial ones of non-rivalness in consumption and non-exclusion possibility of non-payers. I build upon the partial insight of Samuelson to claim that the three concepts of private, public and merit goods are ideal concepts which can be present jointly and in varying degrees in every economic event. Given that both Samuelson and Olson show the need for the government to make, in some cases, a decision without sufficient scientific evidence (Samuelson) or on ethical considerations (Olson), I argue that the concept of public goods demands the ethical concept of merit goods as introduced by Musgrave. I provide the different definitions and justification given by Musgrave. A discussion of the secondary literature allows me to strengthen Musgrave's own confession that he has only been able to give a partial justification of the concept of merit goods. I announce that in the next chapter I will provide a Kantian inspired justification for merit goods.

Keywords • Public goods • Merit goods • Non-rivalness in consumption • Non-exclusion possibility • Ideal concepts • Samuelson • Olson • Musgrave • Leadership/learning • Interdependence of utilities • Redistribution

3.1 Introduction

In his enthusiasm for the new economic order Adam Smith concentrated on the production of private goods with his primary example being the production of pins. But Adam Smith also drew attention to two different kinds of goods: public works and education. Adam Smith, as intelligent of an economist as he was,

---

In this chapter, particularly Sect. 3.3 on "The need for the concept of 'public goods'", I borrow, with some changes, from: Ver Eecke 1999. Available at SSRN: http://ssrn.com/abstract=350220 or http://dx.doi.org/10.2139/ssrn.350220.

W. Ver Eecke, *Ethical Reflections on the Financial Crisis 2007/2008*,
SpringerBriefs in Economics, DOI: 10.1007/978-3-642-35091-7_3,
© The Author(s) 2013

started a descriptive analysis of these two kinds of different goods. Public works such as roads, for instance, are in contemporary economic theory discussed as cases of public goods. Education, which is mostly cost-free and compulsory, is discussed, since Richard Musgrave, as a case of a merit good.

Indeed, Adam Smith says about public works (such as roads) that they are very useful for the whole of society, but "it can never be for the interest of any individual [...] to erect and maintain them [...] because the profit could never repay the expense." (Adam Smith, 651). Hence, Adam Smith sees a role for the government which may use general revenue to pay for these roads. He advises, though, that the expense of public works such as roads may be best paid for by those "who consume such goods" (Ibid.). He gives as an example of such a method of financing public works "the turnpike tolls in England" (Ibid.). This intelligent description of the provision of public works contains the beginning if not the essential elements of modern economic analysis of public goods. However, modern analysis of public goods is more sophisticated.

Adam Smith justifies the role of government in the provision of education by totally different arguments. He writes: "A man without the proper use of the intellectual faculties of a man, is, if possible, more contemptible than even a coward, and seems to be mutilated and deformed in a still more essential part of the character of human nature" (Adam Smith, 740). Adam Smith does not use the argument of self-interest or the profit motive to justify free or subsidized provision of education. Indeed, he explicitly states: "Though the state was to derive no advantage from the instruction of the inferior ranks of people, it would still deserve its attention that they should not be altogether uninstructed" (Ibid.). Instead he uses a moral argument for the justification of providing education without cost: society should not tolerate such deformity of its citizens which results from being uninstructed. As the self-interest of the consumers is not respected, the government cannot expect voluntary payment. For the poorest, payment may not even be possible. Hence Adam Smith proposes that such services be paid by general revenue paid for by the citizens according to their ability to pay. Again we see in Adam Smith's analysis of education the essential elements of the modern economic discussion of merit goods. In that modern discussion we will again find more sophisticated insights.

3.2 The Conceptual Apparatus for Analyzing Economics

The privileged concept for analyzing the economy is the concept of "private good" (e.g.: Samuelson and Temin 1976, 158–161). On the production side, self-interest invites producers to produce the products wanted by the consumers in the most efficient way possible. The competitive market rewards with greater profit the most efficient producers or the producers who provide products not produced in adequate amounts. The competitive market also punishes producers who produce what consumers do not want and collectively punishes those who overproduce certain items. On the consumption side self-interest invites consumers to buy the best products at the cheapest price for what they want to do. Thus, the competitive free market encourages some kind of optimal provision of goods and services for the whole of society even though all actors are pursuing only their own self-interest (Arrow and Hahn, 1).

Some exceptions do emerge, though. As we have already mentioned a competitive free market based on self-interest has difficulty providing public goods in optimal amounts and it allows the provision of (de)merit goods in quantities that are morally objectionable. We find in the work of John Head and Mancur Olson, Jr. sophisticated analyses of the concept of public goods (Head 1974; Olson 1965, 1983). Musgrave and his commentators introduced in the latter part of the twentieth century the concept of (de)merit goods (Ver Eecke 2007, 19–70).

I believe that my contribution, as a philosopher of economics, is to focus on the nature of these three concepts for an analysis of the economic reality. Thus, I like to claim that the three concepts of private, public and merit goods are not taxonomic concepts, i.e., concepts like house, chair or table. Rather, I wish to argue that these three central economic concepts point to characteristics of economic events. Hence, an economic event can be both a private and a public good or a public and a merit good or even a private, a public and a merit good.[1] Furthermore, the three economic concepts of private, public and merit good are to some extent idealized concepts. Hence, the concepts can be applied in degrees (Samuelson 1969, 108–109; Musgrave 1959a, 8; Musgrave 1959b, 88; Ver Eecke 2007, 23 and 29).

Some economists have pointed to some of these ideas but have created unsolvable paradoxes or contradictions by only pointing to some but not all the above characteristics of the three concepts.

Thus, Samuelson acknowledges that the concepts of private and public goods refer to polar or ideal cases. But then he remarks about the relation between public and private goods with the following: "'A public good is one that enters two or more persons' utility'. What are we left with? Two poles and a continuum in between? No. With a knife-edge pole of the private-good case, and with *all* the rest of the world in the public-good domain by virtue of involving some 'consumption externality'" (Samuelson 1969, 108–109). It thus looks like the concept of private good would become useful only for a "knife-edge pole of private-good cases" only (Ibid). The power of being an ideal concept (and thus applicable in degrees to the whole field of reality) is limited to the idealness of the concept of public good.

---

[1] "The suggested distinction between private and social want [public goods] is not of an absolute sort. Inefficiencies arise in the satisfaction of private wants through the market process, and wherever such is the case, one could say that an element of social want is involved' (Musgrave 1959a, 8; Ver Eecke 2007, 23). "Note that consumption choices which are supported [merit goods] or penalized [demerit goods] may involve goods which are private (rival in consumption) as well as goods which are social (non-rival) [i.e., public goods]" (Musgrave and Musgrave 1984, 78; Ver Eecke 2007, 51).

The ideal concept of private good is seen as powerless in its application. Happily, Samuelson corrects himself and restores the application power of the ideal concept of private good when he writes: "the useful terminology in this field should be: pure private goods in which the market mechanism works optimally, and possibly close approximations to them, versus the whole field of consumption-externalities or public goods" (Ibid.).

Similarly, Musgrave originally created a paradox when he argued that the concept of merit good is intimately connected with the concept of public good. He writes: "note that the benefits derived from such services [free education or hospital services] [i.e., merit goods] extend beyond the specific beneficiary, and thus approach what I have described as the central type of social wants [i.e., public goods]" (Musgrave 1957, 111; Ver Eecke 2007, 21–22). But later Musgrave notices that some merit goods, such as low-cost housing and free milk, are subject to the "exclusion principle" (Musgrave 1969a, 12; Ver Eecke 2007, 33) and are thus private goods also. Thus in one place Musgrave claims that merit goods are public goods. In another place he claims that they are private goods. As the concept of private good is not the same as the concept of public good this seems contradictory. In his latest publications Musgrave solves this contradiction by explicitly stating that merit goods can be also both either private or public goods (Musgrave 1971, 313–314; Ver Eecke 2007, 37). As Musgrave also argues that a good can be partially private and partially public (footnote 1), we find in Musgrave the arguments for our claim that the three concepts of private, public and merit goods are not taxonomic concepts but concepts referring to aspects of economic goods.

If we combine and highlight the conclusions of my reading of both Samuelson and Musgrave we can state that the whole of economic reality can and must be analyzed by considering the applicability of the three ideal concepts of private, public and merit good.[2] Only the claim that the concept of merit good too is an ideal concept is not in the texts quoted from either Samuelson or Musgrave. In order to unify the understanding of the three crucial concepts of economics I am prepared to make that claim myself.

3.3 The Need for the Concept of "Public Goods"

Economists use mathematics and geometry for their analysis of private goods. In both their mathematical and geometric analysis they assume the possibility of continuous change in quantities. This assumption presupposes the infinite divisibility

---

[2] "Common pool resources" could be considered a necessary fourth concept (Barkin & Shaumbaugh). But Samuelson's ideal concept of public goods defines public goods as quantitatively having "a condition of *equality* rather than of summation" for all consumers (Samuelson 1955, 350). Hence, Samuelson's concept of public good explicitly captures "common pool resources."

of private goods (Arrow & Hahn, 61). This assumption of infinite divisibility is not a realistic assumption. Chairs and tables lose their identity once they are split up. The assumption of infinite divisibility is thus an exaggeration or an idealization of the fact that private goods are available in a great amount of different quantities. But there are goods which are not available in different quantities. I can buy one, two, three or even more slices of toasted bread for breakfast. Most regions have only one airport. Most streets have often only one bridge over a river. Between cities there is mostly only one highway. Thus, analyzing economically the provision and buying of bread must present different problems than analyzing the economic justification of building an airport. This comparison leads us to a central difference between private goods and other goods. Private goods are characterized by divisibility. The other goods are characterized by lumpiness or indivisibility. They are labeled "public goods."

By the above argument we have pointed to economic events that do not fit the definition of private goods. By giving these concrete examples the name "public goods," we gave the impression that the word "public good" is a tag for a series of concrete economic events. This is often the common sense use of the concept "public goods." In the history of economic thought we see a search for the meaning of the word "public goods." That meaning leads to the creation of an ideal content attributed to the word "public goods."

3.3.1   The Characteristics of a "Public Good"

A first step in searching for the meaning of the concept "public good" consists in pointing to different characteristics observed in economic events labeled "public goods." In *Public Goods and Public Welfare,* Head enumerates the following characteristics as features used in the economic literature to define public goods: (1) decreasing costs in production, (Head 1974, 176) (2) externalities, (85) (3) Samuelsonian joint supply, (77 ff.) (4) non-exclusion, (80) (5) non-rejectability, (82) (6) benefit spillovers, (271) (7) unenforceability of compensation, (185) (8) indivisibility, (161) (9) non-appropriability, (28) (10) non-rivalness in consumption, (78) (11) economies of scale, (179) (12) multiple user good, (79) and (13) lumpiness, (168). Head wrongly rejects (14) Marshallian joint supply (78–79). Other authors add: (15) free rider possibility, (Buchanan 1975, 207), (16) non-subtractability, (Ostrom and Ostrom 1991, 165–167), (17) the fact of not being packageable, (Ostrom, et al. 1991, 140) and finally (18) the strategy of holding out (Ostrom and Ostrom 1991, 170). There are, therefore, at least eighteen terms referring to characteristics of economic events with public good aspects. However, some of the eighteen characteristics are obviously related to each other in as much as they point to the same aspect, albeit from somewhat different angles.

The second step in searching for the meaning of the concept "public goods" requires grouping the above-enumerated characteristics with the purpose of arriving at a single definition of the concept "public good." I will first reduce the 18 characteristics to four groups (I to IV) which I then will show to point to two basic features of "public goods" (A & B).

3.3.1.1 Four Groups of Characteristics

Group I. Violation of infinite divisibility theoretically required by the concept "private good".

(8) Indivisibility: This concept means that certain goods are not available in all desirable quantities, but only in specific sizes.

(15) Lumpiness is a synonym for indivisibility (Head 1974, 168).

Group II. One good, many users. Decreasing cost possibilities.

(3) Samuelsonian Joint supply: In order to avoid confusion, one should distinguish between Samuelsonian and Marshallian joint supply. The term 'Marshallian joint supply' refers to a situation where two or more products are necessarily produced by one process, such as meat and wool from sheep (Bannock et al. 1972, 239; Head 1974, 78–79). This concept belongs in the discussion of public goods only if there is unenforceability of compensation of one of the jointly produced services. The term 'Samuelsonian joint supply' refers to a situation where, because one product can be enjoyed by many, it becomes efficient for consumers to join together in the production process. Samuelsonian joint supply is, thus, a production reaction to a characteristic of the consumption condition (Head 1974, 77).

(12) Multiple user good: Sharp introduced this term to avoid the confusion that is possible with the term "Samuelsonian joint supply".

(10) The term non-rivalness in consumption conveys the same characteristic as Samuelson's concept "joint supply". The only difference is that this term describes the characteristic from the point of view of consumption and not of the solution in production. This concept also means to convey the same characteristic as the one referred to by Sharp's term "multiple user good". The difference is that Sharp describes the characteristic from the point of view of the economic good under consideration and not from the point of view of consumption of that good.

(1) Decreasing production costs simply refers to the fact that there are economies of scale (Bannock et al. 1972, 135–137). Head, however, looks at the possible effects on consumers of decreasing production costs. He points out that a major consequence of economies of scale for consumers is that each additional consumer buys not only a rival good (a car or a PC), but also provides, at the same time, a positive externality for all other consumers of this good: i.e., a lower unit price for the car or the PC (Head 1974, 28, 176–179). Economists can thus look upon the case of decreasing production costs or economies of scale as a case in which consumers are confronted with a rival good that also has an externality that is non-rival in consumption (i.e., the price at which the rival good can be offered given the quantity of the rival good demanded, which is strongly correlated with the quantity of consumers demanding the rival good). According to Head the cheaper price of a PC resulting from an increase in demand for PC's is similar to

the cheaper cost requested from consumers resulting from an increase in consumers for goods generally recognized as public goods, such as bridges and lights in back alleys. For the study of the concept of public good, the relevant aspect of decreasing cost in production is therefore the positive externality of lowering the price for all consumers by the mere fact of buying an additional unit of the rival good or, in other words, the non-rival consumption gift of a lower price for a rival good resulting from any increase in demand of the rival good. Thus, the fixed costs for the production are shared by more persons when there is a greater demand for the good.

(11) Economies of scale are the cause of decreasing production costs per unit with increase in demand. Economies of scale are relevant for these results in that they produce something for the consumer. I analyze the different aspects of this phenomenon under the term 'decreasing costs in production' in the previous paragraph.

(16) Non-subtractability which is defined as the fact that "consumption by one person precludes its use or consumption by another person" (Ostrom and Ostrom 1991, 165–167). Such a good is thus completely rival in consumption. A completely non-subtractable good is a good where joint consumption takes place without the crowding out effect. It is thus completely non-rival in consumption. If the good is partially subtractable we face partial non-rivalness in consumption where there is partial loss in enjoyment from additional consumers.

Group III. Not internalizing the price of an aspect into the price of the total good.

(2) Externalities are costs and/or benefits from consumption or production that are not reflected in market prices (Bannock et al. 1972, 158–159).

(6) Benefit spillovers, according to Head, refer to positive externalities resulting from the provision of services by one jurisdiction that are enjoyed by residents of another jurisdiction (Head 1974, 270–278). Clearly, this concept is a subcategory of the concept "externalities". It restricts the beneficiaries to lower-level governmental jurisdictions.

(7) Unenforceability of compensation is understood by Head as the central characteristic of externalities (Head 1974, 185–186).

(5) Impossibility of rejection is defined by Head as an extreme form of external diseconomy (Head 1974, 83).

(14) The term Marshallian joint supply refers to a situation where two or more products are necessarily produced by one process, such as meat and wool from sheep (Bannock et al. 1972, 239; Head 1974, 78–79A). Head provides an argument for treating this case as consisting of private goods that can be handled in a Pareto-optimal way by the market and therefore does not belong to the problematic of public goods (Ibid.). If we take another example, that of the beekeeper, then we have the case of one product or service that is paid for (honey) and another service (pollination of the apple trees leading to increased apple production) that is jointly supplied but where compensation is unenforceable. Marshallian joint supply can therefore present a public goods problem if one jointly supplied service is such that compensation is unenforceable.

Group IV. Payment problems: the inability to prevent enjoyment without pay.

(7) Non-exclusion is a term used to describe the enviable position of a consumer who can enjoy a product without having to pay for it. This situation arises when a producer or a consumer has no economically sensible method of excluding another consumer from enjoying the good or service without the latter paying his/her share in the good or service that s/he co-consumes.

(17) The fact of not being packageable is defined as the impossibility "of being differentiated as a commodity or a service" (Ostrom and Ostrom 1991, 140–141) so that "it can be readily purchased and sold in the private market" (Ibid.) and where "those who do not pay for a private good can then be excluded from enjoying its benefits" (Ibid.). Political scientists who use the term "packageable" identify the idea with the exclusion principle of economists (Ibid.). In my view, the word "packageable" points to a possible strategy to make the exclusion principle work.

(15) A free rider is a person who makes use of the advantages of the non-exclusion situation (Buchanan 1975, 37, 148). Malkin and Wildavsky claim that individuals "indicate a more honest revelation of preferences than that predicted by free rider theory" (Malkin and Widavsky 1991, 336). However, they overstate their claim when they conclude that it is a fictitious problem. Other authors counter this claim by pointing to experiments that "offer persuasive evidence that free riding is a real phenomenon" (Adams and McCormick 1993, 113). These other authors also point out that "less-than-total free-riding do[es] not demonstrate that the free-rider problem is not prohibitive" (Ibid.).

(18) Holding out is one strategy that a free rider may use (Ostrom and Ostrom 1991, 170). Holding out can be justified by claiming that one has no interest in the public good, less interest than is actually the case, or by disputing the fairness of one's assigned payment. The crucial factor is that the arguments are used in order to refuse participation in financing the public good. When holding out is possible, one is in the presence of a public good.

(7) Non-appropriability is a term used to describe the problem from the point of view of an economic good. Head defines it as "that property of a good which makes it impossible for private economic units, through ordinary private pricing, to appropriate the full social benefits (or be charged the full social costs) arising from their production or consumption of that good."

3.3.1.2 Reduction of the Four Groups of Characteristics to Two Central Features of the Concept "Public Goods"

Let us now reflect more formally on each of the four groups of characteristics of public goods.

Group I includes indivisibility and lumpiness. These two terms are essentially synonymous

Group II includes Samuelsonian joint supply, multiple user good, non-rivalness in consumption, non-subtractability, decreasing production costs, and economies of scale. The first four concepts are essentially synonymous, describing a single characteristic seen from four points of view. The term "multiple user good" describes the characteristic under consideration from the point of view of a good which has special features in its consumption possibilities: it can be used by many consumers and, thus, possesses the characteristic of non-rivalness in consumption. This is the case, because enjoyment of the good by one consumer does not subtract from the usefulness of that good for another consumer. The good is therefore said to be non-subtractable. In consuming such a good, consumers are not rivals. Samuelsonian joint supply is an efficient production strategy for goods with the special consumption feature of non-rivalness in consumption. Head proposes the fifth term "decreasing production costs" as the most general term. Decreasing costs can be obtained from the production side and from the consumption side. The former is, in economic literature, called "economies of scale." The latter is labeled with one of the four essentially synonymous terms mentioned above (i.e., Samuelsonian joint supply, multiple user good, non-rivalness in consumption or non-subtractability). I have interpreted decreasing costs in production and economies of scale as creating a possibility of a non-rival gift of cheaper pro-unit costs for a good with each increase in demand of the good. When a greater number of units are produced then the fixed cost is shared among more units. Thus the fixed cost part of the price diminishes.

Group III includes externalities, benefit spillovers, unenforceability of compensation, impossibility of rejection, and Marshallian joint supply. The relationships among these characteristics can be presented as follows. Externalities can be either positive or negative. In the former case, they are often referred to as "external economies" while in the latter they are often called "external diseconomies." A special form of external diseconomy is the impossibility of rejection. A particular form of external economy is the spillover benefit of local government actions onto non-residents or people outside of the political locality. Another particular form of external economy is a Marshallian joint supply in which the producer of one service has no way of charging a fee for a second jointly supplied service. Externalities are a problem because the price of an aspect of a good cannot be included in the price of the good itself. Thus, there is a price internalization problem. Until the price internalization problem is solved, there is the problem of unenforceability of compensation.

Group IV includes non-exclusion, free rider possibility, non-appropriability, non-packeagability, and the possibility of holding out. These terms too emphasize a same characteristic from different angles. Non-exclusion possibility focuses on the fact that non-paying consumers cannot be excluded from the enjoyment of a good or service. Non-packageability focuses on a characteristic of goods that make exclusion difficult or impossible (i.e., the good is not neatly packageable so that it can be sold in separable units). Lack of packageability of a good or impossibility of exclusion means that consumers can enjoy a good without paying or, in other words, they can be free riders. "Free rider" is, thus, a term for non-paying consumers of goods that are not packageable or that are non-exclusive. A strategy to become a free rider of such goods utilizes holding out voluntary payment by exploiting the fact that one cannot be excluded from enjoying the good anyway.

These four groups can now be further combined. Combination A includes Groups I and II. Combination B includes Groups III and IV.

Combination A: Group I and Group II are related as a cause is related to an effect. Indivisibility or lumpiness is one of the reasons for economies of scale or for the availability of decreasing costs, i.e., of an opportunity for gain.

Combination B: Group III and Group IV are related to each other because the problem with externalities is at bottom the unenforceability of compensation. This concept is closely related to the concept of non-exclusion or non-appropriability.

As a consequence, we are left with the idea that the eighteen characteristics can be reduced to two combinations: Combination A and Combination B. Combination A stresses the opportunity for gain resulting from the existence of goods that can be used by many. This characteristic can then be elevated to an ideal level. Instead of stressing that a good can be used by many, we now can say that for that good there is non-rivalness in consumption. Combination B stresses the problem related to the realization of the opportunity for gain: unenforceability of compensation because of non-exclusion possibility. This non-exclusion possibility can be treated as a technical problem; namely, the problem of finding barriers for non-paid consumption (such barriers include toll-booths, TV signals that are usable only with a descrambler, and taxation schemes). The non-exclusion possibility can, however, also be elevated into an absolute problem. This is the case when barriers cannot be found or when implementing barriers is too expensive. Thinking of non-exclusion possibility as being without a perfect solution is equivalent to elevating it into an absolute and, thus, an ideal level.

Thus, the eighteen characteristics by which public goods aspects or problems are described can be reduced to a related pair:

(1) Decreasing costs from multiple users, thereby offering an opportunity for gain.
(2) Unenforceability of compensation because of non-exclusion possibility. This makes financing the opportunity for gain difficult, if not impossible.

3.3.2 How to Deal with "Public Goods?"

The concept "public good" is a multidimensional concept because it captures two characteristics. Authors looking for solutions for the potential, but unrealized, gain present in public goods can address either one of the two characteristics. Samuelson addressed the non-rivalness in consumption. Olson addressed the non-exclusion possibility. But in both cases the authors take for granted that the solution must respect the wishes of the consumer. Hence, ideally, no consumer should feel worse off after the ideal provision of the public good. If the government is asked to intervene, as in the proposal by Samuelson, the role of the government is to help consumers achieve a potential gain they cannot achieve by themselves alone.

3.3.2.1 Samuelson: The Non-Rivalness in Consumption

As the primary characteristic for his analysis, Samuelson selects decreasing cost resulting from the fact that there are multiple users. From this he is able to derive, with the assumption of self-interested behavior, an optimal level of provision. In the case of a positive economic good, the optimal level of provision is bigger than the sum of quantities that the consumers would individually buy. Left to the free market, public goods will, in that model, be under-provided. There thus exists an opportunity for economic gain with reference to public goods not naturally captured by the free market.

Samuelson includes the second characteristic (unenforceability of compensation) in his analysis when he looks for a method to realize the opportunity for gain. Samuelson's proposal consists of two steps (Samuelson 1954, 387–388 "Optimal Conditions"). First, he asks that the government inquire about how much each citizen is willing to pay for a particular public good (e.g., a bridge). If an entrepreneur is willing to provide the public good at a price that is less than what the citizens are jointly willing to pay, then there is an opportunity for gain for all in the provision of that good.

Second, the government must use its tax power to force people to pay what they declared they were willing to pay. Samuelson uses the government to overcome the unenforceability of compensation. He then points out that citizens will realize that their declared willingness to pay for a public good will be used twice by the government: once to decide whether or not to provide the good and once to decide how much to tax citizens for a particular good. Thus, claims Samuelson, citizens will have a selfish incentive not to reveal their true preferences. Consequently, he concludes, an ideal solution exists, but it cannot be found and realized by the government.

Even at the ideal level, the concept of public good represents a difficult-to-realize opportunity for gain. It is difficult to get the information about the desirability of the public good. Or, in economic jargon, there is a problem of true preference revelation.

Nevertheless, even without perfect knowledge, the government must decide whether or not to provide the public good. It also must decide how much of the public good it should provide. Finally, the government must decide, all without completely trustworthy information, on a tax schema. Under such circumstances, it is not possible for the government to reach an optimal solution and a Pareto distribution of taxes for the public good. What justification does the government have to decide? If the concept of "public goods" does not provide the full justification, economists will have to look for another concept. I will argue that the concept of "merit goods" provides a possible justification.

3.3.2.2 Olson: Impossibility of Exclusion

Olson is an author who does not look for the government to realize the opportunity for gain present in public goods. He studies the conditions under which individuals acting out of self-interest will provide a public good. The crucial characteristic of public goods that will act as a disincentive for paying voluntarily is the non-exclusion possibility (i.e., even if one does not pay one cannot be excluded from enjoying the public good once it is provided). Notwithstanding this disincentive, public goods are sometimes provided voluntarily by collective action financed by dues or fees. The solutions for overcoming the disincentive of non-exclusion possibility are different in small, medium and large groups.

Olson mentions three methods to overcome the problem of providing a public good in a small group. One person might have enough interest in the public good to alone finance the good, as in the case of a family with teen-age daughters wanting the safety of a light in the back alley. If the most interested person is not willing to pay alone, he might create social pressure by organizing a social gathering and proposing a burden-sharing where the holdouts are socially embarrassed. Finally, the person most interested in the public good might demonstrate to all the participants that a minimum contribution of each is required to collect enough for the provision of the public good. The most interested person, the leader, makes the members of the small group aware of the undeniable connection between their contribution and the provision of the good. The non-exclusion possibility is dealt with in this last case by demonstrating that the non-exclusion possibility will not apply since the good itself will not be provided if everybody does not contribute or does not contribute enough. Bargaining is still a possibility, but it is diminished by the logically demonstrated possibility of non-provision in case of lack of payment.

For medium groups, it is unlikely that the first strategy, that of one person paying the total cost of the public good, will occur often. The other two strategies can still be used: social pressure (a list of contributors to the church organ is published) and demonstration of connection between payment and provision (a publication of total cost, payments received and assigned payments to reach the goal of, say, building a new parish center). Holding out and underpayment remain possible strategies, but the potential gains created by the non-exclusion possibility are made less attractive by the creation of social pressure and individual guilt.

With large groups (workers interested in safety in the workplace or citizens interested in preserving the ozone level) the two remaining strategies that could be used in groups of medium size lose much of their importance. Indeed, the connection between the payment of one individual and the provision of the public good is almost non-existent (the payment or non-payment of union dues by one worker will not change the prospect of better safety laws; similarly, the contribution of one citizen will not measurably change the ozone level). The paradox with public goods for large groups is that the payment of dues or fees for the public good by any one person is both personally significant (union dues are substantial) while it is insignificant with reference to the total cost of the public good and, thus, to the level of additional provision and additional enjoyment. It is, therefore, not economically rational for members of large groups to pay for their public good. But, if all members of the group follow their private economic rationality, then the public good for the group will not be provided. Paradoxically, private rationality leads to collective irrationality.

Olson observes that some groups are able to provide their public good not-withstanding the logical difficulties just described. Olson then asks the question: How do they do it? Olson argues that the successful provision of a public good for large groups consists of a two-step process. First, the potential beneficiaries of the public good must be mobilized. The latent group must become an active group. Second, the active group can then pursue its public goods (unions may seek legislation promoting work safety). In order for a latent group to become mobilized into an active group, there needs to be a leadership that articulates the goals of the group. Articulating the goals of the group is not sufficient for overcoming the disincentive created by the non-exclusion possibility for public goods benefitting large groups. Individuals simply do not have the personal incentive to voluntarily contribute to public goods that benefit large groups (Olson 1965, 44). The leadership, thus, needs to create private incentives associated with the membership in the large group (Olson 1965, 132). The leadership of some groups have natural incentives available (decrease of price for malpractice insurance for physicians becoming members of the AMA) while leaders of other groups must rely on more artificial incentives (Christmas parties, picnics, credit unions). In both cases, the mobilization of the latent group into an active group requires that the selective incentives for joining the group are large enough to motivate the individual members to pay their dues or fees to the group. The dues or fees can then be used to provide the public good for the group.

Several critical remarks can be made about the voluntary provision of public goods by the mobilization of latent groups using private incentives. First, the solution is not optimal because the provision of the public good is not determined by its usefulness but, instead, by the success or failure to mobilize the latent group. If the mobilization fails, then the good will not be provided. If the mobilization succeeds, then the public good will tend to be overprovided because the willingness to pay dues is not limited by the usefulness of the public good, but also, if not mainly, by the attractiveness of the selective incentives which are often unrelated to the primary public good targeted. If the mobilization of the latent group succeeds, there is overabundance. If it fails, there is famine.

A second critical remark concerns a suggestion of Olson about large groups that fail to mobilize themselves. Olson suggests that it might be the case that the mobilization of a group is the easiest, if not the only, way to realize the provision of a public good (work safety laws promulgated under the pressure of unions). Might it not be justified for the government, so Olson asks, to create artificial incentives for the relevant latent group so that they can mobilize themselves, and thus, become the engine for the provision of a desirable public good? Through legislation—authorizing union shops or closed shops—the government can create a legal situation that provides workers who want work, with private incentive to join unions. Olson understands that his suggestion involves the use of the government's coercive power as part of the strategy to promote the provision of certain public goods. Accepting coercive power for the provision of a public good rests on the meritorious judgment that the public good is worth the loss of some degree of freedom. This is not a purely economic analysis whose recommendation is justified because it is Pareto optimal. Instead, it is a recommendation based upon the declaration that a good—in this case a public good—is also a merit good.

3.4 The Concept of "Merit Goods"[3]

Implementation of public goods policies led us to claim that merit judgments were part of such implementation strategies.

Musgrave introduced officially the idea of meritorious judgments in economic theory by creating the concept of "merit goods." He introduced the new concept because he observed that some economic events such as free medical treatment for the poor and subsidies for low-priced housing (Musgrave 1956, 341; 1969a, 143; Ver Eecke 2007, 20 and 31) were at that time without full conceptualization.[4] Indeed, it is the case that both private goods and public goods are expected to be fully paid for. Thus those two examples and the ones Musgrave added later cannot be conceptualized as private or public goods. Even the idea of transfer payments did not fully explain his two examples because the transfer payments were accompanied by the restriction that the recipient could not use the transfer funds for what the recipients wanted. The transfer funds could only be used for what the

---

[3] In this section on merit goods I borrow from Wilfried Ver Eecke."Introduction" *in An Anthology Regarding Merit Goods*. West Lafayette. Purdue University press, 2007.

[4] Later Musgrave added additional examples such as free education (Musgrave 1957, 111, 1959a, 13; Ver Eecke 2007, 21, 24), publicly furnished school luncheons (Musgrave 1959a, 13; Ver Eecke 2007, 23), free milk (Musgrave 1969b, 12, 1971, 313; Ver Eecke 2007, 33 and 37) or milk for babies (Musgrave 1969a,143; Ver Eecke 2007, 31), "food, shelter, health and so forth. ... earmarked (specific) subsidies which assure equality in consumption of necessities (Musgrave1969a, 143-44; Ver Eecke 2007, 32), free dental clinics (Musgrave 1971, 313; Ver Eecke 2007, 37) "a specified basket of goods, e.g., essential items of food, clothing, and shelter [linking it to "categorical equity"] (Musgrave and Musgrave 1984, 99, 1996,187; Ver Eecke 2007, 53 and 70), "programs in support of child care" (Musgrave and Musgrave 1984, 512; Ver Eecke 2007, 55), "future consumption" (Musgrave 1987, 452; 1990, 207–208; Ver Eecke 2007, 57 and 62), "Concern for maintenance of historical sites, respect for national holidays, regard for environment or for learning and the arts" (Musgrave 1987, 452; 1990, 208; Ver Eecke 2007, 57 and 62), "The role of merit goods [...] bears some relation to the philosophers concept of "primary goods" (Musgrave 1987, 453; Ver Eecke 2007, 58). He also gives examples of demerit goods like "penalty taxation, as in the case of liquor (Musgrave 1959a, 13; Ver Eecke 2007, 24); "prohibition of sale of dangerous drugs or sumptuary taxes (Musgrave 1969b, 11; Ver Eecke 2007, 33); "Penalty taxes ... imposed on liquor or tobacco (Musgrave 1971, 313; Ver Eecke 2007, 37; see also Musgrave and Musgrave 1976, 328; Ver Eecke 2007, 46); "pornography" (Musgrave and Musgrave 1976, 66; Ver Eecke 2007, 46); "taxes, including those on narcotics, adulterated butter, and wagers, are imposed" (Musgrave and Musgrave 1976, 328; Ver Eecke 2007, 47; also Musgrave and Musgrave 1984, 438; Ver Eecke 2007, 54); "Restriction of drug use or prostitution as offenses to human dignity" (Musgrave 1987, 452, 1990, 208–209; Ver Eecke 2007, 58 and 62).

community deemed meritorious enough. To fill the gap in conceptualization, Musgrave created the concept of "merit goods." Musgrave gave several definitions of the concept of "merit goods." Here are the crucial ones; (1) "Where interference with individual preferences is desired" (Musgrave 1956, 340; Ver Eecke 2007, 21). (2)"when the majority decides that certain wants of individuals should be satisfied, even though these individuals would prefer to be given cash and use it for other purposes" (Musgrave 1957, 111; Ver Eecke 2007, 21). (3)"where public policy aims at an allocation of resources which deviates from that reflected by consumer sovereignty" (Musgrave 1959a, 9; Ver Eecke 2007, 23). (4) "The reason, then, for budgetary action is to correct individual choice" (Ibid.). (5) "The satisfaction of merit wants, by its very nature, involves interference with consumer preferences" (Musgrave Id., 13; Ver Eecke 2007, 24). (6) "In the case of merit wants, however, the very purpose may be one of interference by some, presumably the majority, into the want pattern of others (Musgrave Id., 14; Ver Eecke 2007, 25). (7) "the problem of merit wants, where interference with consumer sovereignty is the crux of the matter" (Musgrave id, 89; Ver Eecke 2007, 28). (8) "From this it may be concluded that society in fact wishes to impose a substantial degree of interference with consumer preference; and that therefore a theory of imposed choice should be incorporated into the fiscal model. Wants with regard to which consumer choice is abandoned and the satisfaction of which is imposed I have referred to as merit wants, and have argued that they remain outside the normative model" (Musgrave 1969a, 143; Ver Eecke 2007, 31). (9) "The recognition of merit wants thus appears to involve substitution of imposed for individual choice and a clear departure from the basic principle of consumer choice" (Musgrave 1969b, 12; Ver Eecke 2007, 33). (10) "In practice, merit wants tend to be associated closely with redistribution (Musgrave 1969b, 82; Ver Eecke 2007, 34). (11) "the idea of voluntary redistribution may go far to explain the prevalence of merit goods. […] Hence majorities may be obtained for redistribution in kind (tyranny of giving), even though redistribution in cash could not be agreed upon. In this way, the importance of merit goods for low-income groups may be explained in terms of voluntary (or semi-voluntary) but conditional giving. […] Outright preference imposition may be intended, but distributional considerations (voluntary or semi-voluntary redistribution in kind) also enter" (Musgrave 1971, 317–318; Ver Eecke 2007, 39). (12) "In certain instances, it appears to be the very intent of the decision maker to interfere with or override individual preferences. […] In the situations now considered, such interference is not accidental but the [p. 81] very purpose of public policy. Certain goods are held meritorious (they are considered "merit goods") while others are held undesirable" (Musgrave and Musgrave 1973, 80–81; Ver Eecke 2007, 42; Musgrave 1976, 65; Ver Eecke 2007, 45). (13) "Thus the existence of merit goods is linked to voluntary redistribution" (Musgrave and Musgrave 1976, 66; Ver Eecke 2007, 46). (14)"Selective taxes may be imposed to discourage the consumption of "demerit" goods. [..] Such taxes, though they tend to be highly regressive, are supported on "sumptuary" grounds, be it because the consumption of such products is considered immoral or unhealthy. Society decides to interfere with consumer choice, and to treat such items as demerit goods" (Musgrave and

Musgrave 1976, 328–329; Ver Eecke 2007, 46). (15) "While the state or community "as such" cannot be the subject of wants, a distinction between private and communal concerns of individuals cannot be rejected that easily. Nor can the role of communal concern be resolved in the utilitarian frame by allowance for interpersonal utility interdependence. There remains an uneasy feeling that something is missing. The concept of merit wants (Musgrave and Peacock 1958; Musgrave 1987) and of categorical equity (Tobin 1970) address this gap, but much remains to be done to resolve the problem of communal wants in a satisfactory fashion" (Musgrave 1996, 187; Ver Eecke 2007, 70).

Commentators observed that Musgrave, over time, produced a series of definitions of the concept of merit good which place emphasis on different aspects of merit good. Thus, an early commentator, McLure, argued that the primary emphasis in Musgrave's definition of the concept of merit good was the "interference with" or the "violation of" individual preferences (McLure 1968, 474; Ver Eecke 2007, 74).[5] Head, on the other hand, argued that the primary emphasis of Musgrave's definition of the concept of merit good was "the correction of individual preferences" because "preference distortion problems constitute the essence of the merit wants concept" (Head 1988, 4; Ver Eecke 2007, 118).[6] I agree with McLure. I see in the idea of "correction of individual preferences" an attempt to provide a justification for at least some merit good policies. But a justification presupposes a prior problem. I see that prior problem in the "interference with individual preferences." Interference with individual preference is a problem in economic thinking because economic activity is understood to have as purpose to satisfy individual wants and wishes not to interfere with them. Musgrave devoted much effort to try to find forms of reconciliation for the apparent interference with individual preferences. He was aware that his arguments for reconciliation were not fully satisfactory. Particularly with reference to demerit goods Musgrave sees a sharp opposition between societal wants and individual wants. Hence, I see the essence of Musgrave's concept of merit good in the idea that many economic events include a clash between individual wishes and societal decisions, policies or regulations.

Musgrave does specify a limit to the justifiable use of the new concept. Thus he writes: "Interferences with consumer choice may occur simply because a ruling group considers its particular set of mores superior and wishes to impose it on others. Such determination of wants rests on an authoritarian basis, not permissible in our normative model based upon a democratic society" (Musgrave 1959a, 14; Ver Eecke 2007, 24). I agree in this point with Musgrave.

---

[5] Musgrave uses the word "interference" explicitly in definitions 1, 5, 6, 7, 8, 12 and 14. Musgrave uses the word "impose" in definition 8, 9, 11 and 14.

[6] Musgrave uses the word "to correct" only once in the above enumerated definitions: i.e., in definition 4. However, when Musgrave looks for reasons to justify merit good interventions by the state he uses the idea that consumers do not have enough information, are mislead by advertisements and thus he uses the idea of correction of consumer preferences as a justification for merit good policies.

After having presented his arguments for merit goods Musgrave confesses at the end of his career that the concept remains problematic (Musgrave 1996, 187; Ver Eecke 2007, 70). I interpret that to mean that Musgrave is unable to provide a complete justification for the concept; he is only able to give partial justifications. Let me survey these partial arguments and give them a popular name:

(1) There is the *ethical* justification or definition of the concept merit good. Musgrave points to the fact that authorities make the judgment that some goods are meritorious or demeritorious and therefore aim at increasing or decreasing the level of consumption.

(2) There is the *political* justification of the concept. In this case Musgrave refers to the political system which has the power to make decisions about economic matters. Musgrave then distinguishes between different motives or reasons for the political interference in the economy.

(a) I wish to label the political interference in the economy a *Marxist* one if it is made in the self-interest of a governing elite or of a dictator. Musgrave explicitly rejects this definition and justification of concept of merit goods.

(b) I wish to label that interference a *paternalistic* one if it is made by a well-intentioned (political) elite.

(c) I wish to label that interference a *democratic* one if it is made by a democratic majority imposing its will on the minority.

(d) I wish to label that interference a *republican* one if the interference is justified and limited by the *leadership-learning* theory. In this case the idea is that a society can benefit from leaders who use their superior information to teach the citizens by forcing them to consume goods (or to consume at levels) that they otherwise would not, in the conviction that the citizens will thereby have the opportunity to discover for themselves the benefits of these goods. After a certain time, it is expected that the citizens will agree with the political decision previously experienced as interference.

(3) There are the *anthropological* reasons for justifying merit goods. They point to deficiencies in the consumer: lack of knowledge, lack of evaluating capability, and weakness of the will. As a consequence, Musgrave argues, there is room for correcting consumer preferences.

(4) There is the *sociological* justification which affirms that society has values which might be different from those of individuals. Hence there is a clash between the preferences of society and those of individuals. Sometimes it is argued that the clash between individual and societal preferences derives from interpersonal utility dependence (e.g., A likes it when B consumers education, even if B does not). Here Musgrave reduces the concept of merit goods to public goods arguments.

(5) There is the *liberal* definition, whereby merit goods are defined as public goods whose public good characteristics are not easily visible. As these merit goods are considered to be public goods economists can argue that the government is only helping individuals realize their own preferences, which is the role that the liberal tradition assigns to the government.

(6) There is the *mixed* definition. Here merit goods are said to be private goods handled by the government as if they were public goods.

(7) Lastly, there is the *redistribution* theory of merit goods. Here Musgrave observes that the West seems to have made a bargain. The West is willing to tolerate the inequalities in wealth generated by the free market provided that it is coupled with some measure of redistribution. When the redistribution is not made by cash-transfers but by subsidies in kind, then we are in the presence of merit goods (redistributive merit goods). These redistributive merit goods (subsidies in kind) do not just aim at general equity, they aim at categorical equity: i.e., they aim at securing the satisfaction of specific categories of needs (e.g., physical needs which require food, clothing, shelter and health services).

What is Musgrave's own evaluation of these different justifications? There are several constant themes. First, Musgrave rejects firmly the Marxist justification of merit goods as unacceptable. It violates both the economic norm of consumer sovereignty and the political norm of democracy. Second, Musgrave timidly affirms the validity of merit goods. To an imaginary opponent who would defend "a position of extreme individualism [and] could demand that all merit wants be disallowed" (Musgrave 1959b, 13), Musgrave does not reply with epistemological arguments that demonstrate the falsity of the opponent's position. Rather he replies with a mild moralistic position: "that is not a sensible view." (Musgrave 1959b, 13) A mild moralistic disapproval is not the same as an epistemological rejection. None of Musgrave's arguments is therefore, in Musgrave's own opinion, able to refute an extreme individualist. As modern economic theory is rooted in the assumption of individualism, Musgrave cannot be said to have solved the tension within economic doctrine created by his new concept of merit good.

What are some of the shortcomings of the different justifications offered by Musgrave? First, there is the ethical justification. This justification simply states that an ethical judgment is made, that some good is declared meritorious. But clearly the right for such a declaration, the right for such a judgment is to be defended.

Second, there is the political justification. Since the Marxist approach is rejected, we are left with the paternalistic, the democratic, and the republican justifications. A paternalistic justification, described as the decision by an elite with good intentions, is not necessarily a decision that is economically optimal. The economic profession has the right to analyze any political decision, including paternalistic ones, from an economic point of view. Political justification is not economic justification. As is well known, the economic analysis of paternalism in redistribution leads to the conclusion that such paternalism is inefficient because redistribution in cash is more efficient than redistribution in kind. Some authors, though, present sophisticated counter-arguments and thus support provision of certain goods below market price (Burrows). Next, the democratic justification consists in accepting as politically legitimate the procedurally correct expression of the wishes of a majority. Here the work of Brennan & Lomasky is illuminating. But clearly, the will of the majority, even if expressed in a procedurally correct way, may not be economically optimal. Again, a political justification is not an economic justification. Finally, the republican justification uses the leadership-learning argument to justify merit goods. This is a potentially valid argument. However, the argument requires that the forced consumption be limited to the time minimally required for the citizens to learn the good qualities of the merit good in question. Where there is no such time limit, there the interference extends beyond what is justifiable.

Third, there is the anthropological justification, which argues that concrete human beings do not have the knowledge, the judgmental capabilities, and the strength of will postulated by pure economic theory. But do these limitations not also pertain to governmental bodies? This justification does no more than create a possible opening for merit goods. Here the work of John Head was foundational but it does not fully justify them.

Fourth, the sociological justification simply states that there is a difference in social and individual preference. That does not justify yet which preference should prevail. Clearly, societal preferences can be deficient, inferior, or even wrong.

Fifth, there is the liberal justification, which justifies a merit good because it has public goods characteristics that are not easily visible. This argument points to intersubjective dependencies of personal utilities. This argument was elaborated by Cay Folkers. But if the concept of merit good is understood as consisting of public good characteristics why even create a new name?

Sixth, there is the mixed definition, which calls a merit good the governmental attitude of treating private goods as if they were public goods. This relies on an attitude of the government which at first sight looks not only unjustified but plainly wrong. If something is a private good then economic theory tells us that the competitive free market is the place where the transactions should take place. The government is supposed to stay out of such transactions. For there to be an economic justification for government intervention a serious reason has to be provided. Saying descriptively that the government treats a private good as a public good is no conceptual justification at all for government intervention.

Seventh and last, the merit good argument based on redistributive intentions is in Musgrave's text rooted in the simple descriptive observation that in the West there seems to be a moral bargain: on the one hand, allowing great difference in wealth and, on the other hand, demanding a minimum of redistribution. The moral bargain is not argued for and we therefore have no idea how great the redistribution should be. Furthermore, some economists argue that cash redistribution is more efficient than redistribution in kind. For this argument to work, arguments in favor of categorical equity are required. Categorical equity is mentioned—but not argued for—by Musgrave.

I like to start from the insight of Musgrave in his later writings: the concept of merit or demerit good finds its basis in the existence of two sources of wants: the individuals and society. Instead of trying to reconcile these two kinds of wishes, I like to accept the idea that these two kinds of ideas might be in conflict. I accept the primacy of individual wishes. I therefore see it as my task to derive the need for social wishes from individual wishes. I will do so by asking what the possibility conditions are for making the world of individual wishes and its realization reasonable. I hereby rely on the Kant's method of reasoning where he asked what the possibility conditions were for the existence of objects and for the meaningfulness of the moral world. If we apply this reasoning to world of economic goods and individual wishes we are able to argue that the possibility for satisfying individual wishes is the fact that individuals have access to desirable economic goods. As economic goods are useful for the satisfaction of the desires of many individuals we can expect a form of Hobbesian fight of all against all for economic goods, unless there is (over)abundance. In order to avoid a war of all against all individuals need the help of society. This help takes the form of creating property rights in which society guarantees individuals the exclusive right to some economic goods provided individuals respect the right of other individuals to the exclusive right to those economic goods which society has defined as their property. For this system to work individuals have to respect society's property decisions or society has to create a mechanism to enforce its decisions against those individuals who object to them.

Such an interpretation of merit goods makes societal intervention a necessary condition for the possible reasonable fulfillment of individual wishes. In the next chapter I will argue that a well functioning economy needs eleven domains in which reasonable merit and demerit goods decisions should be made. I hereby expand the domain of the concepts of merit and demerit goods beyond what Musgrave himself articulated. However, Musgrave himself steadily expanded the domain in two ways. First, he found more and more examples of merit and demerit goods.[7] Second, Musgrave included in his later writings whole categories of merit and demerit goods with almost infinite application possibilities. Thus for merit goods he pointed to the series of government efforts to increase consumption of merit goods justified by the argument of leadership/learning, of the interdependence of utilities and of redistribution (Musgrave 1971, 314 and 316; Ver Eecke 2007, 38–39). For demerit goods, Musgrave refers to the whole group of sumptuary taxes or even regulatory taxes (Musgrave and Musgrave 1973, 80; 1984, 438; Ver Eecke 2007, 42 and 54). Thus my expansion of the applicability of the concepts of merit and demerit goods, which I will argue for in the next chapter, is in the spirit of Musgrave's own work.[8]

---

[7] See footnote 4.

[8] John Head, the author who has most extensively written about the problem of merit goods, agrees with me when he writes in his review of my Anthology Regarding Merit Goods: "From his introduction to the volume, it is clear that Ver Eecke regards the merit goods concept as having much wider application than Musgrave himself has ever suggested. He argues this very persuasively on a case-by-case basis in summarizing the contributions from a wider literature in Part III of the volume. With this view, I would emphatically concur" (Head 2008). For a good summary of my views expressed in the same anthology, see Henningsen 2007. I wish to report that Musgrave himself in a telephone conversation agreed with my expansion of the applicability of the concept of merit goods.

References

Adams RD, McCormick K (1993) The traditional distinction between public and private goods needs to be expanded, not abandoned. Am J Political Sci 5(1):109–116

Arrow KJ, Hahn FH (1971) General competitive analysis. Holden-Day, San Francisco

Bannock G, Baxter RE, Rees R (1972) The penguin dictionary of economics. Penguin Books, New York

Buchanan JM (1975) The limits of liberty: between anarchy and leviathan. University of Chicago Press, Chicago

Head JG (1974) Public goods and public welfare. Duke University Press, Durham

Head JG (1988) On merit wants: reflections on the evolution, normative status and policy relevance of a controversial public finance concept. Finanzarchiv, N.F. 46:1–37 (Also published in Rationality, Individualism and Public Policy. Brennan G and Walsh C, Eds. Canberra: Australian National University, 1990, 211–244)

Head JG (2008) Review of: Wilfried Ver Eecke, an anthology regarding merit goods. Purdue University Press, West Lafayette 2007. http://www.amazon.com/Anthology-Regarding-Merit-Goods-Unfinished/dp/1557534284/ref=sr_1_3?s=books&ie=UTF8&qid=1343652299&sr=1-3&keywords=Ver+Eecke

Henningsen K (2007) A great econ book for any discipline. http://www.amazon.com/Anthology-Regarding-Merit-Goods-Unfinished/dp/1557534284/ref=sr_1_3?s=books&ie=UTF8&qid=1343652299&sr=1-3&keywords=Ver+Eecke

Malkin J, Wildavsky A (1991) Why the traditional distinction between public and private goods should be abandoned. J Theor Politics 3(4):355–378

McLure CE (1968) Merit wants: a normative empty box. Finanzarchiv, N.F. 27(2):474–483

Musgrave RA (1956) A multiple theory of budget determination. Finanzarchiv, N.F. 17(3):333–343

Musgrave RA (1957) Principles of budget determination. In: Joint Economic Committeee (ed.) Federal expenditure policy for economic growth and stability. Government Printing Office, Washington, pp 108–115

Musgrave RA (1959a) The theory of public finance, Musgrave at Michigan University. McGraw-Hill Book Company, New York

Musgrave RA (1959b) The theory of public finance, Musgrave at Harvard University. McGraw-Hill Book Company, New York

Musgrave RA (1969a) Provision for social goods. In: Margolis J, Guitton H (eds) Public economics. Macmillan Press Ltd., London

Musgrave RA (1969b) Fiscal systems. Yale University Press, New Haven

Musgrave RA (1971) Provision for social goods in the market system. Public Finance 26:304–320

Musgrave RA (1976) Adam Smith on public finance and distribution. In: Wilson S (ed.) The market and the state. essays in honor of Adam Smith. Oxford University Press, Oxford pp 296–319

Musgrave RA (1987) Merit goods. In: Eatwell J, Milgate M, Newman P (eds) The new Palgrave: a dictionary of economics. Macmillan, London

Musgrave RA (1990) Merit goods. In: Brennan G, Walsh C (eds) Rationality, individualism and public policy. The Australian National University, Canberra, pp 207–210

Musgrave RA (1996) Public finance and finanzwissenschaft traditions compared. Finanzarchiv, N.F. 53(2):145–193

Musgrave RA, Musgrave P (1973) Public Finance in theory and practice 1st edn. McGraw-Hilll Book Company, New York

Musgrave RA, Musgrave P (1976) Public finance in theory and practice 2nd edn. McGraw-Hilll Book Company, New York

Musgrave RA, Musgrave P (1984) Public finance in theory and practice 4th edn. McGraw-Hilll Book Company, New York

Musgrave RA, Peacock AT (eds) (1958) Classics in the theory of public finance. McGraw-Hill Book Company, New York

Olson M Jr (1965) The logic of collective action. Schocken Books, New York

Olson M Jr (1983) The political economy of comparative growth rates. In: Muller DC (ed.) The political economy of growth. Yale University Press, New Haven

Ostrom V, Ostrom E (1991) Public goods and public choices: the emergence of public economies and industry structures. In: Ostrom Vincent (ed) The meaning of American federalism. Institute for Contemporary Studies, San Francisco

Ostrom V, Thiebout CM, Warren R (1991) The organization of government in metropolitan areas: a theoretical inquiry. In: Ostrom V (ed.) The meaning of American federalism. Institute for Contemporary Studies, San Francisco

Samuelson PA (1954) The pure theory of public expenditure. Rev Econ Stat 36:387–389

Samuelson PA (1955) Diagrammatic exposition of a theory of public expenditure. Rev Econ Stat 37:350–356

Samuelson PA (1969) Pure theory of public expenditure and taxation. In: Margolis J, Guitton H (eds) Public economics. Macmillan Press Ltd., London

Samuelson PA, Temin Peter (1976) Economics. McGraw-Hill Book Company, New York

Smith A (1937) The wealth of nations. The Modern Library, New York

Tobin J (1970) On limiting the domain of inequality. J Law Econ 13:263–277

Ver Eecke W (1999) Public goods: an ideal concept. J Socio-Econ 28(3):139–156

Ver Eecke W (2007) An anthology regarding merit goods. The unfinished ethical revolution in economic thought. Purdue University Press, West Lafayette

Chapter 4
Business Ethics and Eleven Categories of Merit Goods

Abstract In this chapter I add the concept of merit goods to the concepts of public goods and the free rider problem as one more economic concept that can be useful in the vocabulary of business ethics. Musgrave defines merit goods as goods that are so meritorious that the government has the right to interfere with consumer preferences. Thus the government can subsidize education and even make it obligatory. Musgrave (and I agree) stresses the fact that the concept of public goods is quite different in that in the provision of public goods the government intends to respect the wishes of consumers. I then produce a Kantian argument to justify and limit merit goods and I defend eleven categories of merit goods. I provide an example of a failed merit good implementation. The food business was successful in preventing the government's implementation of the merit good program for breast feeding. Our question is whether, and when, business leaders have the obligation not to try to stop the implementation of a proven merit good. At the end of the chapter I argue that the idea of merit good expands the notion of stakeholder beyond what the concept of public good is doing.

Keywords Business ethics • Financial crisis 2007–208 • Breast feeding • Ethical conflicts • Public goods • Categories of merit goods • Property rights • Economic efficiency • Education • Safety net • Public health measures • Well-functioning social contract • Transparency • Strategic planning • Environmental protection

4.1 Introduction

Business ethics is well acquainted with the importance of certain economic concepts for its discipline. Public goods and the related concept of free rider problems are eminent examples. In this paper I wish to introduce another economic concept—merit goods—as having the promise of becoming crucially important for the field of business ethics. Richard A. Musgrave, a Harvard professor in public finance, introduced the concept fifty-seven years ago and defined merit goods as goods or wants "[w]here interference with individual preference is desired"

(Musgrave 1956, 340; Ver Eecke 2007, 21). Musgrave gives as reason for interference in the case of merit goods the fact that these goods or services are: "considered so meritorious that their satisfaction is provided for through the public budget, over and above what is provided through the market and paid for by private buyers" (Musgrave 1959a, 13; Ver Eecke 2007, 23). Musgrave identified public subsidies for housing, subsidized and obligatory education, obligatory inoculation and free hospitals for the poor as meeting the definition of this new economic concept, (Musgrave 1956, 340; Ver Eecke 2007, 20).[1] Conversely, the government may choose to impose a tax or create regulations to diminish the consumption of certain "demerit goods" that individuals consume excessively (e.g., taxes on alcohol, tobacco; regulation of drugs). (Musgrave 1971, 313; Ver Eecke 2007, 37).

This paper argues that the concept of merit good allows us to articulate conceptually when an ethical conflict exists for business leaders between their fiduciary duty to their primary stake-holders and their more general and ambiguous duty to the common good. While a potentially difficult topic for the discipline, it is also a very pertinent one since lawmakers around the world develop policies that appear to impede consumer sovereignty more frequently.[2]

Section 4.2 begins with an example of where the government failed to provide a merit good because business leaders successfully used their political power to block it. Section 4.3 argues that the idea of merit good is a necessary economic concept by stressing the insufficiency of the concept of public good to clarify a number of economic events. Section 4.4 presents a philosophical argument for the concept of merit good and its many categories. Section 4.5 lays out the eleven categories of merit goods justified by our economic and philosophical arguments. Before concluding I reflect in Sect. 4.6 on the applicability of the concept of merit good for business ethics.

---

[1] For a list of the growing examples of merit and demerit goods in Musgrave's writings see footnote 4 in Chap. 2.

[2] A current example of such trend in the United States are government bans on trans fat, with major cities like New York and Philadelphia outlawing their use because of obesity and other health concerns (Jennifer Steinhauer 2008). In 2008, California became the first state to ban trans fat in restaurants and over 20 states currently have bills pending in their legislature to enact similar bans. Kiera Manion-Fischer, "States Consider Trans Fat Bans, menu labeling", Stateline.org available at http://www.stateline.org/live/details/story?contentId=383615 (accessed Nov. 9, 2009). For the past several years, the European Union has debated a Union-wide smoking ban and many countries have already enacted it. The Health Secretary in Britain has gone so far as to advocate that smokers and overweight individuals be denied state-funded medical operations until they get fit. Oakeshott, Isabel, "Hewitt: Smokers Should Stop before They're Treated" The Times Online http://www.timesonline.co.uk/tol/news/uk/health/article1364697.ece (accessed November 9, 2009).

4.2 Merit Goods and Ethical Conflicts in the Business World

In 2007, the Washington Post described how the formula industry successfully stopped the government's attempt to increase breast-feeding among women. Breast-feeding provides health benefits for children with little to no risk. It is "associated with fewer ear and gastrointestinal infections, as well as lower rates of diabetes, leukemia, obesity, asthma and sudden infant death syndrome" (Kaufman & Lee, A4). Although beneficial to children, breast-feeding rates in the United States remain low and lag behind those of many European nations (ibid.). Breast-feeding thus fits Musgrave's definition of a merit good because it is an important good which is under-consumed. In 2004, Federal health officials decided to intervene and attempted to increase breast-feeding. They "commissioned an attention-grabbing advertising campaign [...] to convince mothers that their babies faced real health risks if they did not breast-feed. The campaign featured striking photos of insulin syringes and asthma inhalers topped with rubber nipples" (ibid., A1). According to the Washington Post, the infant formula industry took at least two steps to deal with the threat to their industry. First, they hired a former chair of the Republican National Committee and a former top regulatory official to lobby the Department of Health and Human Services, the agency responsible for the campaign (ibid., A1, A4). Not much later, the breastfeeding ads were substantially toned down, substituting inhalers for dandelions and ice-cream scoops. Shortly afterwards, the lobbyist sent a letter to then HHS-Secretary Tommy G. Thompson thanking him "for his staff's intervention to stop health officials from 'scaring expectant mothers into breast-feeding'" (ibid.). Second, the infant formula industry increased infant formula advertising from about $30 million before the government campaign in favor of breast-feeding to $50 million during the government campaign (ibid.). Breast-feeding by mothers dropped from 70 % before the government and industry campaigns to 63.6 % after the campaigns in 2006 (ibid., A4).

The merit good campaign to increase breast-feeding in 2003–2005 thus failed. This case study demonstrates a general question for business ethics: If the government presents valid arguments for an important merit good, is it morally acceptable for a businessman to fight the work of merit good implementation on the grounds that it is a threat to one's own company's profitability?[3] I propose that knowledge of important merit goods adds an additional dimension to the moral and ethical problems faced by business leaders. It is true that business ethics has the concept of common good to identify similar ethical challenges. However, the economic concept of merit good presents new arguments because it relies on economically justified programs supporting the common good.

---

[3] We do not address here the ethical problems connected with bureaucrats and politicians accepting the influence of lobbyists. Lobbyists sometimes contribute important knowledge. Other times lobbyists use methods of influencing which can be considered unethical.

4.3 Economic Justifications of Merit Goods

Everybody, including business ethicists, should take seriously the concept of merit good because the concept is necessary to explain and justify the provision of those public goods which demand interference with consumer preferences. If the interference with consumer preferences is intended then the good cannot be considered a public good and there must be a new economic concept to describe the event and I argue it is the concept of merit good. Alternatively, if the interference with consumer preferences is considered regrettable then, I will argue, one needs a non-public good's argument to justify the regrettable aspect of the implementation of public goods policies. That novel argument again is a merit good argument.

When Richard Musgrave first wrote about merit goods, he observed that several economic goods and services(e.g., publicly furnished school lunches, subsidized low cost housing, free education) could not be subsumed under the two super-concepts of economic theory: private and public goods.[4] Such goods and services, he reasoned, are neither pure private goods[5] nor pure public goods.[6] What Musgrave calls merit goods cannot be considered private goods because, under current economic thinking, free competitive markets are the best way to maximize the utility of private goods for all consumers and distribute the benefits fairly. Thus, free school lunches cannot be considered private goods. If they were handled as private goods then the market would be used to provide them. The market would establish a price at which willingness to buy and willingness to produce and provide would find an equilibrium. One might regret that not enough people can buy sufficient amounts of lunches as one can regret the many limitations imposed on human beings by there being limited budgets. To regret the consequences of the market mechanism is one thing. But when the government selects some goods and services and decides to do something about the regret by, for instance, providing the school lunches for free then we have a new situation.

---

[4] For a discussion of both the development of Musgrave's understanding of the concept of merit good and a survey of the secondary literature, see Ver Eecke 2007.

[5] Private goods are goods that can be transacted through voluntary contracts by individuals who are able to exclude its use by others and whose utility is rivalrous. Consumption by one consumer prevents shared utility by another. By consuming a private good, say an apple, a shoe or an automobile, others cannot enjoy it.

[6] Musgrave stresses that the difference between a private and a public good (social good in Musgrave's terminology) is one of degree. "In the case of private wants, the divergence between private and social product is a more or less marginal matter; in the case of social wants, the divergence becomes of the essence. Private wants are provided for adequately by the market. Social wants must be satisfied through the budget if they are to be satisfied at all. For purposes of public policy, the difference in degree thus becomes an important difference in substance." (Musgrave 1959a, 8; Ver Eecke 2007, 23).

A decision has been made to change the results of the free market distribution for these goods.[7]

However, these so-called merit goods are not public goods either. Public goods are necessary in economic theory because certain goods are non-rival and non-excludable, requiring collective action (voluntary or forced) for their provisions.[8] This explanation of government intervention (enforced payment for instance of highways by toll booths) is not sufficient to justify free school lunches and mandatory inoculation. Under public goods' theory, public goods can only be provided if individuals are willing to pay for them. Providing free school lunches violates this principle because those receiving the food are by definition unable to pay. Mandatory inoculations are contrary to the theory of public goods because willingness to pay in order to receive inoculation is not a factor in deciding to vaccinate everyone. With both free lunches and mandatory inoculation, the government is not helping individuals overcome collective action obstacles—the foundation of public good theory. Instead, the government interferes with consumer's wishes because the free market does not distribute these goods to as many people or in sufficient quantities as is morally or socially desirable.[9]

---

[7] The concept of merit good introduces ethical decisions in economics. This contradicts the view that economics is a positive science (Friedman 1953). Hence, several economists, such as Charles McLure and Aaron Wildavsky, object to the concept of merit good (McLure 1968; Wildavsky 1987; Ver Eecke 2007, 73–113; 85–113).

[8] Either the good is so expensive that no individual can pay for it but it is still useful for society (say a bridge) or it might be affordable on an individual level but no one will spend the money because they are discouraged by the free rider problem. Non-excludability leads to the free-rider problem. The free-rider problem describes a situation where a non-buyer can enjoy utility from a good or service without paying for it. For example, if a family installs a streetlight in a dark alley, any passerby will reap the benefits of the increased safety without having to pay for it. Moreover, the fact that others feel safe would not diminish the safety of the buyer of the light. If collective action does not take place, a market failure occurs. Suppose there are three families whose houses face the same ally. All want to install a streetlight in the ally for public safety. Family A is willing to pay $100 for the light, Family B is willing to pay $300 and Family C is willing to pay $400. If the cost of the light is $600 then no single family would be willing to buy it even though the cost is less than the $800 combined utility. Hence the combined utility is not realized. Thus, the problem with (pure) public goods is that, often, no individual has an incentive to buy or provide these goods, and even less to buy or provide them in the optimal amount. If the cost was less than $400 but more than $300 then Family C has self-interest to buy it while A and B do not but could still enjoy it, highlighting the free-rider problem. However, if collective action is taken, the group can buy the light even if it costs more than $400 because all three are willing to contribute. Thus, a collective decision (voluntary or forced), instead of the free market, can optimize the provision of these goods because it is able to force would be free-riders to pay their share of the cost. Note however that the government is merely a facilitator to ensure consumer choice can be fulfilled. This is all the more true if the number of potential consumers increases.

[9] Musgrave says it as follows: "The satisfaction of merit wants cannot be explained in the same terms as the satisfaction of social wants. While both are public wants in that they are provided through the public budget, different principles apply. Social wants constitute a special problem because the same amount must be consumed by all, with all the difficulties to which this gives rise. Otherwise, the satisfaction of social wants falls within the realm of consumer sovereignty, as does the satisfaction of private wants. The satisfaction of merit wants, by its very nature, involves interference with consumer preferences" (Musgrave 1959a, 13; Ver Eecke 2007, 24).

Moreover, in some cases the implementation of public goods requires government intervention, violating consumer's wishes. Hence, just as the presence of externalities in private goods demanded a new concept—public goods—when the externalities became too big, the need for a non-voluntary interference with some consumer wishes in the implementation of public goods requires the new concept of merit good.

Andel has argued that public goods also often involve government interference with consumer sovereignty, implying that there is no need for the concept of merit good (Ver Eecke 2007, 242). But, by examining two theories of public goods implementation, either by means of governmental action discussed by Samuelson or by voluntary collective action advocated by Olson, I will solidify our claim that the implementation of public goods introduces the need for the new concept of merit goods.

Paul Samuelson developed the first theory of public goods and proposes that the government must ask all citizens how much they value a particular service or good (e.g., a new bridge, free swimming pools, police protection). If the sum of the declared value for all citizens together is greater than the cost, then the state should provide the good or the service. The state should use its power of taxation to raise the money to pay for the good or service. Advocating the state's use of the power of taxation to pay for a public good is Samuelson's method of dealing with the free rider problem. The state must, however, only charge each person according to his declared utility in the good or service. In a state where the only taxes would be the requested payment for the desired public good and where the taxes would never be more than the amount which the citizens themselves declared they were willing to pay it looks as if the taxes are not experienced as imposed. Instead they are experienced as an exchange of a voluntary payment for a desired (public) good. Hence Samuelson's approach to the provision of public goods is sometimes called the voluntary exchange theory of taxation (Head 1974, 153 ff). Under such an argument, it is clear that the state performs only a subservient role in the provision of public goods since it does so with the intention of respecting consumer wishes (Samuelson 1954, 1955). The government is needed in this case only because public goods have technical characteristics that make it difficult for individuals to acquire them in an optimal way because of the free rider problem, among others. Even so, the wishes of the consumer citizens remain sovereign. No interference is intended in Samuelson's approach.

However, on closer inspection the role of the government becomes more complicated given, first, that consumers out of self-interest might declare less interest in the public good than they really have, so as to minimize their payment for the public good and, second, that the government can use its power both of eminent domain to confiscate needed property when the owner does not want to sell and its power of taxation even when opposed by some citizens.[10] In both cases declared

---

[10] The Fifth Amendment to the U.S. Constitution provides "nor shall private property be taken for public use, without just compensation". U.S. Const. amend V. This requires only that the government pay for property it takes; it does not prohibit the government from taking property an individual wishes to keep. The Supreme Court recognized this government right to seize property in the 1875 case *Kohl v. United States*. 91 U.S. 367 (1875).

self-interest is overruled which is contrary to the pure theory of public goods. These government actions demand a merit good argument.

Under Samuelson's schema, the government can only charge each individual according to his or her declared utility of the good. It is not difficult to assume that many individuals, once they see the connection between their declared utility and the amount they have to pay, would intentionally underestimate the utility of a certain good. It is worthwhile to make explicit the implications of this theorem. Indeed, it means that using information about public goods from economic agents, to whom one ascribes self-interest as the economic motive, cannot be assumed to be true and thus lead to the optimal economic desired result.[11] The government, however, must make decisions even though economic science, based, as it is, on unreliable information obtained from consumers, cannot fully guide it in the domain of public goods. The government must therefore make judgments. But in the absence of true information about citizens' preferences, the government's judgment about the provision of public goods includes guesses, which means consumer sovereignty does not always trump. The Samuelsonian impossibility theorem implies that a choice between subsidies for food stamps, subsidies for highways or subsidies for cancer research includes more than objective information. Economics is incomplete unless it uses at least implicitly ethical value preferences to make choices between the many public goods the government can provide (Stretton and Orchard, 184 ff). Furthermore, the government cannot rely on voluntary contributions for the financing of public goods. It must make use of its power. That power takes the form of "power to tax." Decisions that are not based fully on information and that need the use of force to be implemented, clearly have an ethical aspect, particularly if a subset of consumers object to being taxed for an objectionable public good such as defense for pacifists.[12]

An important alternative approach in realizing the collective action required for public goods is the one proposed by Mancur Olson. Olson asks the question, when will people voluntarily contribute to the provision of a public good? His answer, assuming the individualistic assumptions underlying the free market, is that an individual will freely contribute to the provision of a collective good only if her contribution increases the provision of the collective good by so much that her increased enjoyment of the public good is worth more to her than her contribution. For example, a laborer will voluntarily pay union dues only if the increased services provided to her by the union are worth more to her than her dues. If, however, a worker receives the same wage and benefits as a union worker, then the worker paying union dues does not augment significantly enough the power of the union to increase her wages by more than if she did not pay her dues. Still, if all

---

[11] This is referred to as the Samuelson Impossibility Theorem (Samuelson 1954).

[12] This is the merit good aspect of imperfectly implementing public goods. Libertarians demand a very high standard (survival of the nation is at stake) for accepting that the government's use of the power to tax is justified (Schmidtz 1991, 159). We find such a high standard unreasonable as a condition for implementing public goods policies.

workers did not pay their dues, and thus acted rationally according to the principle of self-interest, all workers would be worse off. A similar argument can be developed for clean air or quality control of food. Individual rationality thus leads to a loss for all. Olson then asks how a society can solve this paradox, within the individualistic framework.

His answer is that the above paradox can be solved by the mobilization of the group of individuals who can benefit from the collective good. This mobilization can occur if individuals are given private incentives that are equal to or bigger than their contribution. These private incentives can be directly related to the collective good pursued by the group (e.g., increased wage benefits) or it might be only marginally or not at all related to the principal collective good (Olson 1968, 51, 133–134).[13] It might now be possible for some groups to find enough incentives to mobilize their group. For others it might not be enough. If the group cannot mobilize itself, then the collective good that the group could buy will not be provided even if every member of the virtual group would be better off, according to their own calculus, if the good were bought.[14] In such cases, argues Olson, it is important that the government reflect on whether or not the collective good is important enough to give the group the means, if not the force, to mobilize itself. The government can do so for unions who fight for safety in the workplace by "union shop" or "closed shop" legislation (Olson 1968, 88–89).

Olson's reflections imply that collective goods are not automatically provided. Particularly when large groups of people are involved, it is necessary first to mobilize the group, often leading to the formation of lobbying groups. If the group cannot possibly mobilize itself and it is concerned with an important public good, then, Olson argues, the government should consider the use of legislation (i.e., force) to mobilize the latent group and thus to make the provision of this public good possible. Without using the label, Olson is asking if some public goods are not so meritorious that they are also merit goods, permitting the government to interfere with some consumers' wishes.

What emerges is that the two approaches to the provision of an optimal amount of public goods appeal ultimately to governmental force. Without an appeal to such a governmental force, the economic order cannot reach a proven or desirable economic optimum. This necessary appeal to force strengthens Musgrave's initial observation that some goods possess something more than the qualities of public or private goods and that the additional characteristic is one of ethical dimension.

Musgrave stresses the difference between a public and a merit good precisely on the point of use of force. The theory of public goods requires that those who

---

[13] Examples of incentives that are only marginally or not related to the principal collective good are availability of group health insurance rates, or of group rates for airline tickets, or the possibility of participating in group activities for the children of members of the group. Unions or cultural organizations have indeed used many of these techniques.

[14] Properly provided no one should be asked to pay more than they voluntarily would be willing to pay if market conditions prevailed.

experience negative utility from its provision be compensated. Where compensation is not given, because impractical or because the consumer is assumed to exaggerate the amount of disutility, the theory still requires us to regret the inconvenience of the disutilities, because the provision of public goods intends to improve the situation of some and to make the situation worse for none. Merit goods are another matter. The theory of merit goods does not include the idea that disutilities have to be compensated. Thus policies aimed at lowering the rate of smoking need not include compensation for the inconvenience posed to smokers. Similarly, antitrust legislation does not include compensation for the restrictions imposed on monopolists. Disutilities for some are intended in the very concept of merit good and not so in the concept of public good.[15]

Thus the concept of public goods is, first, different from the concept of merit good and, second, at the margin the concept of public goods requires the concept of merit goods to justify the use of force in the implementation of public goods policies.

4.4   Philosophical Justifications and the Categories of Merit Goods

Pointing out that the concept of merit goods is necessary to conceptualize certain economic events is one way to justify it, but I also want to take a more ambitious tack and show the conceptual necessity of the idea of merit good. If individuals and consumers desire an end, they have to accept the means necessary to achieve it. That is, individuals have to accept the conditions whether agreeable or not, that are necessary for their wishes. This kind of reasoning rests on the insight that there are logical relations in reality, which have validity, even if consumers do not like them.[16] Thus if one needs food, one needs money to buy it or one must be able to grow it oneself or one needs to be able to rely on somebody to give it.

What are the conditions for the possibility of a given good or service that individuals, as economic actors, wish? Western citizens as economic actors wish for a

---

[15] This is the argument used by Musgrave against Andel's attempt to equate public goods with merit goods on the grounds that even public goods also include government intervention. Musgrave's reply is that government intervention in the provision of public goods is necessarily regretted whereas in merit goods it is intended (Musgrave & Musgrave 1973, 80–81; Ver Eecke 2007, 420). This allows the government to look for ways to minimize interventions in public goods (use toll booths; buy and/or pay a market value for the land needed for a road). For merit goods it leads to progressively stronger interventions and restrictions as in the case of prohibition of smoking where at first there was only a warning on packages.

[16] "… they [Kant's shorter works] begin with experience and regress upon its a priori presuppositions or principles without which it would not be possible to have that kind of experience…." In L. W. Beck, "Translator's Introduction" in *Kant* 1956: vii. Where Kant started with experience, we will start with consumer wishes.

free market.[17] In order to prevent individuals from escaping the discipline of the competitive free market, the state will have to impose measures which violate the Pareto principle. These measures are the necessary conditions—the possibility conditions– for implementing the ideal efficiency of the free competitive market. I shall call merit goods those goods that are the conditions for the possibility of the free market, especially if these merit goods or services themselves are not preferred by consumers. Paradoxically, a market left truly free (that is entirely unregulated) will not perform what are considered the beneficial functions of "free markets." Thus, if individual consumers desire a free market they have to accept the necessary conditions to arrive at it even if they seem contrary to their short-term interests. These are what Kant would call conditions of the possibility, or those things necessary, to achieve an end. Describing merit goods this way sets a theoretical limit to the concept. The government cannot thwart the wishes of the consumer whenever it feels like it: the government needs arguments to justify overriding consumer sovereignty. It should only act when its actions will facilitate the market or its effectiveness and its actions are morally and constitutionally acceptable. If this philosophical reasoning is correct it means that economic thinking necessarily has to propose that the government should perform economic activities that interfere with the wishes of consumers. That is, one can assume that economic thinking will propose economic activities to the government, which will respect neither the Pareto principle nor the consumer sovereignty principle. This means that economists will recommend to the government some economic activities, which might cause disadvantage to some citizens, and might favor others.

Thus, the concept of merit good refers to those economic activities of the government that cannot be justified by arguing they help consumers achieve the satisfaction of their wishes. Such activities are captured by the concept of public good. Merit goods can be justified as the necessary conditions for the efficient working of the system (the free market) in which the consumers try to satisfy their wishes and desires. These necessary conditions become merit goods when they are not wanted or are even opposed by some citizens (laws protecting property justifying jailing of thieves). One could argue that this has the potential for circular reasoning: if consumers want to satisfy their wishes, this requires a free market, which Kantian reasoning tells us requires fulfilling certain possibility conditions. The logical progression is that if consumers want to satisfy their wishes it requires accepting all their possibility conditions. The idea of merit good is only needed because individuals do not fully realize the requirements for their wishes or their real desires but potentially—with increased logical capacity or education—they could come to see that the disliked possibility conditions actually conform to their consumer sovereignty. The "paternalism" that merit goods entail is necessary until individuals

---

[17] One could argue that the free market is not a good per se, that it is an institutional or legal arrangement. Still, we want to maintain that institutional arrangements are produced. They involve the use of some resources. They result in something that is desired. In as much as institutional arrangements result in something desirable, they are a good or a service. In as much as they require resources they must be called economic goods.

align their interest with what they really want. Such a suggestion makes it hard to argue that merit goods are as fundamental in economic theory as private and public goods or that they should change the way one thinks about economics.

However, accepting this argument requires the belief that all people can be perfectly rational decision makers and that the self-interest of some will not override the collective interest of the whole. Several economic studies have shown that this assumption about rational choice does not hold since people often lack well-ordered or stable preferences and make different decisions based only on how the question is framed. Gaining more information does not necessarily improve the decision-making process either (Sunstein 1167). The result is that individuals are unlikely to make rational choices because they do not have full information, good judgment or are unable to do what their good judgment says.[18] If rationality is impossible to guarantee in private good transactions, it seems even more difficult to guarantee for the types of decisions necessary to fulfill the possibility conditions for a free market. These conditions are not always obvious and may take a long time to provide the desired effects. Moreover, while merit goods should positively affect the whole, they may not necessarily positively affect each individual, making it even harder to surmount the obstacles to rational choice already well documented. To believe that at some point more education or logical instruction could overcome such basic human drives is unlikely at best. Irrational choices are a fact of life.

Likewise, one cannot assume that everyone will be able to overcome their immediate self-interest and serve the larger societal goal of a functioning free market. Not only is it notoriously difficult for people to put off short-term rewards for long-term benefits, but as a community we are naturally reluctant to satisfy all individual preferences because some cause harm. Thieves must be forbidden to steal property and a small businessman who cannot afford proper waste removal still cannot dump his trash into a lake. In both cases, without enforcement one has little hope of these individuals following the rules that are better for society as a whole but not for them in the particular instance. One sees this type of behavior and, correlatively, necessary enforcement on a larger-scale in the case of monopolies. The natural tendency in a free market is for companies to eliminate competition, leading to sole control over a certain product or sector. The negative results for society as a whole are well known (Simons 1948, 129 and Passim; Smith, 712). Thus, it is widely accepted that this natural tendency of companies must be checked in order to have a more efficient market. We have no reason to believe that the self-interest of individuals and companies could be inhibited by anything other than government enforcement. Since most people will not always make rational decisions and will often pursue their own interests over that of the collective, the argument that merit goods could become public goods once people realize their "real desire" fails.

---

[18] This is the main argument used by Head to reconcile merit goods with the consumer sovereignty tradition in economics. Merit goods, according to Head, are justified because they are trying to realize the true interests of consumers (Head 1966, 3–6; 1969, 215–218; 1988, 4–5; 1990, 214).

4.5 Categories of Merit Goods

Of course, the most pertinent part of this discussion for philosophers and business people alike is to know what the main categories of merit goods might look like if one employs the above definitions. I have consulted the history of economic thought to discover what economists in the past have described and defended as legitimate governmental tasks in the economy (Ver Eecke 1998, 140–144; 2007, 334–337). In the following pages I will systematize the argumentation for the different categories of merit goods by using, as much as possible, a Kantian method of reasoning. I will ask what are the necessary conditions for the possibility of realizing what citizens, as economic actors, wish for? That is, what is necessary to secure an efficient free market?[19, 20] This has led us to argue that one can expect eleven major categories of merit goods in which the government has an important role in providing institutional arrangements for the economy to work properly.

Our eleven categories will be noticeably broad and critics may say too general.

---

[19] We call this method of reasoning Kantian because we see Kant developing both his *Critique of Pure Reason* and his *Critique of Practical Reason* on the basis of two facts whose possibility conditions he wants to understand. For Kant's own summary see: Kant, *Critique of Practical Reason*, 1956, 166–168.

[20] There are at least four other ways of justifying and simultaneously limiting the range of merit goods. A first justification I like to call the search for silver bullets (Burrows 1977, Ver Eecke 2007, 281–294). Burrows argues that some economic goods, such as milk, have the exceptional capability to promote multiple goods. By subsidizing milk, children can be expected to have a healthier diet; the poor will benefit more than the rich form this policy because food is a greater percentage of their budget; the rich will not be jealous because they benefit equally; finally, the redistribution is used for a good cause (provide a better diet) and not for conspicuous consumption (a Cadillac, a TV, expensive sneakers). A second justification is based on the fact that consumers make bad decisions (Head 1966, 1969, 1988, 1990). Head then sees a legitimate place for merit goods as corrections for distorted individual preferences, be it because of lack of information, lack of judgment or lack of will (Aristotle's akrasia) in the consumers. Head also sees that Musgrave gave a distributional role to his concept of merit good. A third justification observes that individuals act differently in the market than in the political arena when they vote (Brennan and Lomasky 1983, 1993). People who drive when drunk might vote for strong penalties for drunken drivers. For Brennan and Lomasky, a merit good is any political vote limiting market behavior. They imply that mostly the political vote is more rational and more moral than market actions. A fourth justification stresses the fact that the consumption of some goods by other people (poor children having breakfast) provides psychic benefits. The presence of such goods creates psychic utility interdependence. If a pure utility calculus would be made we would be in the presence of public goods. Folkers points out that in democratic societies such psychic utility interdependence gives rise to an ethical debate on what should be done. Often a moral consensus deviates from a utility calculus and leads to merit good policies (Folkers 1974; Ver Eecke 2007, 253–280). An overview of the discussion about merit goods can be found in two reviews of my anthology on merit goods (Ver Eecke 2007). The first is by Kate Henningsen. http://www.amazon.com/gp/pdp/profile/A1KGYMOEYD4G45/ref=cm_cr_dp_pdp (Accessed Jan 15, 2010). The second is by John Head. http://www.amazon.com/gp/pdp/profile/A1JF4CHMTPI0W6/ref=cm_cr_dp_pdp (Accessed Jan 15, 2010).

However, our purpose is not to argue for specific policies, but to assert that the government has a responsibility in each of the particular areas. This responsibility can be exercised in myriad ways and within each category the way to implement them should be the least intrusive in order for merit goods to do their job, namely to increase the efficiency and good working of the economy as opposed to paralyzing it.

4.5.1 Defining and Protecting Property Rights Including Granting Limited Liability

Economic actors desire a free market economy because that system maximizes efficiency and, consequently, consumers' utility. This characteristic of the free market is recognized by both defenders and critics of the free market (Adam Smith 1937, 14, 421, 423, 651; Marx 1948, 11–12). However, a free market needs certain rules and restrictions in order to function properly. The most basic system of rules necessary for the free market to work consists of clearly defined and protected property rights along with the necessary legal system to sustain them. Which property to protect and where to assign privilege is not something the market will or can do. If the government did not protect private property rights as well as the economic gains derived from the sale or use of such property, the risk of trade or sale would be too great for most individuals. Few people would gamble away their time or money if there were a likelihood that the profit from such ventures could revert to others. The stipulation of property rights is not just a matter of the past: i.e., a requirement to get the free market started. It is an ongoing process as is evident by the continuing process of enacting patent and intellectual property laws.

Another restriction crucial for a flourishing free market is a restriction that makes it less risky for corporations to make and sell products. It is the concept of limited liability. Without this law I could expect greater caution by corporations to sell certain products.

Securing property rights and imposing on the market limited liability is often regarded as a public good because individuals or corporations have to rely on a central authority to fulfill a desire they cannot do by themselves—protect their things and limit their liability. However, imposition of property rights and guaranteeing limited liability does not respect a crucial aspect of the concept of public good: i.e., respect of the wishes of all participants with the hope and intend that there are no losers. In guaranteeing limited liability there are losers. The same is true for the establishment of property rights as already pointed out by Adam Smith.[21] Property rights necessarily secure certain consumers' desires at the

---

[21] "Civil government, so far as it is instituted for the security of property, is in reality instituted for the defence of the rich against the poor, or of those who have some property against those who have none at all" [Italics are mine] (Adam Smith 1937, 674).

expense of others. Hence, property rights just as limited liability cannot be fully justified with the concept of public goods. I justify both, with the Kantian argument, that they are possibility conditions for the free market. Of course one can ask if the actions taken with regards to property rights and limited liability are efficient, wise, prudent, or even just. All of these questions take the problem of property and limited liability out of the domain of nature (facts, events) and relocate it into the domain of values, which is the defining difference between merit and public goods.

4.5.2 Institutional Arrangements to Promote Economic Efficiency

The second kind of merit good emerges when economists develop a different ontology of the free market. Indeed, Adam Smith described the free market as the "simple system of natural liberty" which establishes itself on its own accord if interferences are prevented (Adam Smith 1937, 651). Smith's ontological view of the free market is that it is a natural system that, once allowed to establish itself, will maintain itself. The neo-liberal tradition, however, argues that Smith's ontology of the free market is naive.[22] The free market is, according to the neo-liberals, not a natural event; it is a human institution that imposes burdens on its participants—e.g., the threat of bankruptcy; the imposition of competition; and the requirement that one needs to pay in order to secure goods. Because it imposes burdens, it is an institution that many want and try to escape. Cartels and trusts were examples of systematic attempts to escape the burden and the limitations of the free market. But why erect an institution that many of its members and many of its most powerful members want to escape? The answer of the neo-liberals is that the free market is a meritorious institution and deserves to be defended because the free market promotes something valuable: efficiency.[23] The neo-liberals therefore locate the free market as a whole in an axiological space. But if an institution is considered to be a necessary instrument for achieving a value, then it is possible to argue that even if individuals do not like that institution, it nevertheless might still have to be maintained. It is this line of argumentation that neo–liberals take when they argue that the government should promote and finance the

---

[22] For a full study of neo-liberalism, see Nawroth 1961. Some important English speaking representatives are: Henry C. Simons, Milton Friedman, Frank A. Knight and F. A. Hayek.

[23] The neo-liberals argue that the free market also promotes certain desirable anthropological virtues such as industriousness, responsibility, reliability, and initiative. They also argue that the free market shows a philosophical predilection for freedom. Finally, they also argue that the free market is conducive to democracy and that a command economy demands a dictatorship. (Ver Eecke 1983, 152; 2008, 78).

enforcement of anti-trust legislation, should work for a stable monetary system,[24] should eliminate subsidies and import duties, should legislate that producers and distributers provide relevant information to consumers and should oppose non-productive activities such as advertisement (Simons 1948, 84–89).[25] At the occasion of economic crises, some economists go back to Schumpeter's idea that a well-functioning economy has a destructive aspect. Bad companies should not survive.[26] Reflecting on the post-communist economies in Eastern Europe Stiglitz

---

[24] Currently a new argument is emerging with reference to regulatory control of banking and the goal of establishing a stable monetary system. The obvious argument is that we have in the US several banks which are too big to fail. Hence these banks can expect that the government will have to bail them out if the risks they toke are threatening their survival. This allows such banks to take excessive risks. If the risk does not materialize they can reap the benefits. If the risks hit them they do not have to pay. They can expect the government to bail them out. Clearly, this situation violates a basic principle of the free market which is that one has the freedom of choice but one must bear the negative consequences just as one may enjoy the benefits of one's choices. This argument of unfairness is made politically potent because it is made by Richard Fisher, president of the Federal Reserve Bank of Dallas (Will). Second, the argument for the breakup of large banks can be made on pure economic grounds. Consider Samuelson when he writes: "'Perfect competition' exists only in the case where no farmer, business man, or laborer is a big enough part of the total market to have any personal influence on market price; on the other hand, when his grain, merchandise, or labor is large enough in size to produce depressing or elevating effects on the market prices, some degree of monopolistic imperfection has set in, and the virtues of the Invisible Hand must be that much discounted" (Samuelson 1967, 41). Samuelson's argument goes beyond the argument "too big to fail" because it argues that even when they do not fail they have the power to escape the rule of free competition and are thus contravening the creation of an optimal economy. This argument is thus an argument of efficiency.

[25] Simons recommends sometimes extreme measures in his 1948 book, but he is, in our opinion, correct in pointing out which areas of the economy require regulations. Thus his statement that advertising adds no value is now seen as extreme. But we now have still a less extreme law: truth in advertising. This law is a restriction of freedom to act as one sees fit in the market. This is precisely the line of argument that Henry Simons and other neo-liberals made. Thus currently, the false advertising law makes it illegal to use, in commerce, any false or misleading description or representation of fact, which "in commercial advertising or promotion, misrepresents the nature, characteristics, qualities or geographic origin of his or her ... goods, services, or commercial activities..." 15 U.S.C. § 1125(a)(1)(B). Under the law, advertising must be truthful and non-deceptive; advertisers must have evidence to back up their claims; and advertisements cannot be unfair. Federal Trade Commission, "Frequently Asked Questions: A Guide for Small Businesses," available at http://www.ftc.gov/bcp/edu/pubs/business/adv/bus35.shtm (accessed Nov. 30, 2009). In enforcing the law, the Federal Trade Commission focuses primarily on ads that make claims about health and safety and ads that make claims that consumers would have trouble evaluating for themselves. Id.

[26] This introduces the idea that the economy should have no companies that are so big that if they fail the economy would suffer so much that the government has to interfere and help such big failing companies. This seems to have been the situation with the financial crisis of 2007–2008 where failing banks were too big to let go under. When JP Morgan suffered billion dollar losses in 2012 the argument of too big to fail was introduced in congressional hearings. Jamie Dimon –JP Morgan's CEO—is quoted as having said: "We can not have too big to fail. We have to get rid of too big to fail so that a bank can fail without doing damage to the economy" (See Rushe:http://www.guardian.co.uk/business/2012/jun/19/jamie-dimon-defends-jp-morgan). Clearly, regulating the economy must include breaking up companies which are considered too big to fail. I thank Christian Rice for providing the evidence of the importance of this argument.

argues that dealing with bad companies requires intelligent bankruptcy laws and intelligent judges.[27] According to Stiglitz what is important is not the right of the creditors or owners but the speed by which the assets can be "re-engaged in productive use."[28]

All measures advocated to make the economy efficient have costs for some economic actors. All economic subjects can, therefore not be assumed, to want such actions. Hence, government activity in these areas cannot be argued for on the basis of public good theory. It can only be argued for as a possibility condition for the efficiency of the free market—the market as promoting a value.

4.5.3 Dealing with Business Cycles

Business cycles by their nature can lead to macro-economic inefficiency such as periods of high unemployment, inflation or recession. John Maynard Keynes argued that it is the duty of the government to improve the market's macro-economic efficiency by creating special measures to counteract the business cycle, particularly recessions (Keynes, 322). Here the government is asked to increase the total demand for goods and services beyond what the market is willing to do such that there is enough demand for goods and service so as to be able to employ (ideally) all those who are willing to work.

Keynes thus gives the government a crucial task in the life of the free market. Fiscal and monetary policies are presented as acceptable–if not necessary–ways for governments to interfere with the market.[29] Again, this role of the government cannot be fully justified on the basis of the public good concept because its policies hurt some and help others. A clear example of the hurt imposed by anti-business cycle policies is the decision to intervene in a period of economic boom. An economic boom increases demand including demand for labor. This increased

---

[27] In the January 7, 2010 WEB issue of *The Economist* a certain Schumpeter wrote an article analyzing the enlightened character of American bankruptcy laws. He applauds the fact that American law distinguishes between potentially viable companies which can file for "Chap. 11" and terminally ill which can file for "Chap. 7." "Chap. 11" allows for restructuring which lets the companies survive. "Chap. 7" aims at liquidating assets. Article available at http://www.economi st.com/businessfinance/displaystory.cfm?story_id=15211818 (Accessed Jan 20, 2010). We thank Goutam Jois for this reference.

[28] Stiglitz (1999) "Whither Reform? Ten Years of Transition." *World Bank*, WEB, 1–32 [Not available anymore]. Quoted in Ver Eecke 2008, 245.

[29] Governments also provide stabilizers that automatically go into effect as the economy declines. One such example is obligatory unemployment compensation. When the economy goes into recession, unemployment compensation payments automatically increase as people become unemployed. Progressive tax systems also have a built in stabilizing effect, taking less percentage wise when incomes fall (during periods of recession) and more when incomes rise (during periods of booms).

demand of labor leads to increase in wages which in turn promotes inflation. High inflation is considered bad for the whole economy. Hence in the name of the good for the whole society the government uses, among others, monetary policy instruments. The Federal Reserve changes the nation's supply of money and the availability of credit in order to decrease spending. One clear consequence is the impact on the wages. They rise slower than without the policy intervention. Still there is a possible justification for the intervention: avoidance of an undesirable rate of inflation. However, this justification rests on a value judgment which expects sacrifices from some. Such a justification does not belong to the concept of public good. It is the definition of the concept of merit good.

The ultimate justification for intervention in the business cycle is long term economic efficiency. Its justification is thus an extension of the argument for our second kind of merit good.

4.5.4 Education[30]

Education is necessary for an efficient economy on two accounts. First, economic analysis assumes that for an efficient economy, consumers must know the characteristics of each product and their prices. Their choices are assumed to be rational but they can only be rational if they are informed choices. Consumers are further assumed to be able to compare the utility of different products. Human beings have innate reasoning power but education dramatically improves their reasoning power by teaching them to read, write, and express their ideas to others. This argument defends education as an instrument for economic efficiency.[31] It can defend educational policies that focus on the three R's: reading, writing and arithmetic.

There is a second reason why education is necessary for the free market and it addresses the humanistic component in education. Indeed, if reaching the efficiency promised by the free competitive market requires governments to impose just regulations on individual activity, then this in turn demands a degree of cultivation of reason in the population. The rationality of citizens, and their ability to process and accept justifiable actions which go against their wishes, becomes the condition for the possibility of the government's ability to impose the necessary regulations to promote an efficient free market. This provides an argument for the support of widespread education, even humanistic education, including education for the lower classes (argument in the nineteenth century) and women (argument in the twentieth century).

---

[30] Universal education is one of the eights "Millenium Development Goals." The eight millenium goals are: 1. End Poverty and Hunger. 2. Universal Education. 3. Gender equality. 4. Child Health. 5. Maternal Health. 6. Combat HIV/AIDS. 7. Environmental Sustainability. 8. Global Partnership.

[31] This argument implies that schools should teach students how to evaluate economic goods and services.

Again the provision of education cannot be fully justified as a public good. If it were, the amount of education would have to be limited to the amount that all, jointly, are willing to pay. Furthermore, education could not be made obligatory, because by definition a public good is desired and need not be made obligatory. This theoretically postulated fourth group of merit goods is not without its empirical confirmation. Christian Scheer has shown that the expansion of the public budget in the latter part of the nineteenth century in all Western societies was in large measure the result of the expansion of payments for education (Scheer, 496 ff.).

4.5.5 Safety Net[32]

Government provision of a safety net for its citizens poses two different questions. First there is the question as to whether or not there should be a safety net and how extensive that net should be. Second, if the safety net is established, the question arises as to how to contain the rising cost, particularly if parts of the safety net are treated as entitlements.

4.5.5.1 Justifying the Provision of the Safety Net

First, the need for a safety net arises from the fact that a competitive free market consists of an institutional arrangement that has a harsh element. Indeed, it is an arrangement in which individuals have a right to a share of the goods and services produced in the economy only if they themselves produce something that others want. If they do not, then the institutional arrangement deprives them automatically of any right to a share of those goods and services. Such individuals are thus faced with bankruptcy, starvation, or both. The purpose of this harsh arrangement is to automatically encourage socially useful productivity.[33]

The goods and services produced in the economy are important because they are necessary instruments for survival, human self-determination, and freedom. The free market economy is considered the best arrangement for the economy to be productive but it is not so capable of guaranteeing the necessary resources to each individual in society. Here the free market needs to be supplemented. Charity is one way of helping those whom the free market leaves out. However, as Hegel

---

[32] End Poverty and Hunger is the first of eight "Millenium Development Goals."

[33] Adam Smith said it this way: "By pursuing his own interest he frequently promotes that of the society more effectually than when he really intends to promote it" (Adam Smith 1937, 423). This is what Smith summarized by his metaphor of the free market as "led by an invisible hand" (Ibid.).

argued, individual willingness to give is full of contingencies. Do the individuals know who is in need? Do individuals, when they know, have the means (Hegel 1967, #242)? With an understanding of the business cycles one can now make a more principled argument: willingness to give is greatest in times of abundance and is the least in times of need. Hence, the existence of business cycles makes that the cyclical nature of charity is out of sync with the cyclical nature of grave need. Individual charity thus needs to be complemented by institutional arrangements organized by the state.

And indeed, it is a fact that Western economies address the possible tragedies that can result from the harsh element of the free market arrangement. Disabled people, the poor, particularly poor children, the unemployed, and the retired all are provided some type of safety net. What is the justification?

As before one can state unequivocally that the concept of public good is insufficient to provide such a justification. That concept could point out that all of us receive some utility from seeing that poor children have some healthy meals. But under the concept of public goods the amount of subsidized food would have to be limited to the amount that the individuals are jointly willing to pay, even if that is nutritionally insufficient. The concept of a safety net includes the idea that the disadvantaged deserve a decent living, regardless of the ability to pay. When the government imposes a safety net that is costlier than the individuals are jointly willing to pay then the government interferes with consumer sovereignty. The gap between the amount consumers are jointly willing to pay voluntarily and the amount demanded by the political process is an amount that cannot be justified by the public good concept. It thus belongs to the idea of merit good to find a justification.

Here our argumentation takes a turn. I cannot use the Kantian argument that the government must impose on consumers those conditions that are necessary for what they want. I was able to create such an argument for property rights, the first kind of merit good. I assumed that the wish for a free market system implied the wish for an efficient free market. This allowed us to develop a Kantian argument for the second, third and fourth category of merit good. The fourth argument included the idea that consumers needed education towards reasonableness. But reason has its own demands. For one, economic efficiency is an instrumental value. It is there for the purpose of doing something with the goods and services we all produce (Ver Eecke 1983, 155–157; 2008, 80–83). Our fifth and following categories of merit goods find their justification in the demands of reason, reason being shown to be necessary in our fourth category.

Here I borrow a vision and an argument from Hegel. He argues that all human institutions are there for the purpose of promoting freedom. Human beings, according to Hegel cannot create freedom alone. They need others. They need institutions. The free market is an institutional arrangement which promotes freedom in many ways. It guarantees individuals the right to make free economic choices. It also promotes efficiency and thus is responsible for eliminating, at least in the Western world, famines. The harsh rule which promotes efficiency is the rule that in the free market one gets no free lunch. The creation of a safety net is providing to some a free lunch. How it is possible to justify the free lunch provided by the safety net?

Here one can look at an analogy in property rights. For Hegel property rights are a necessary instrument for freedom. One can have inner wishes. However, to make these wishes real one needs objects. Thus to realize my wish to be friendly I need to be able to offer, for instance, coffee and cookies. As many people want the same goods, there emerges theft and all kinds of aggression to control objects. A property rights system makes the need for objects more human in that the state guarantees through property rights the access to objects without the overwhelming fear for theft and aggression. With a system of property rights all are more free. Hegel then describes a paradox: the situation of a human being who has no food. Without food he will die. The only food he can have is food he would steal. Hegel argues that the legal system is there to promote freedom. Death is the destruction of freedom. Hence, according to Hegel, in the face of death by starvation property rights cease. The hungry person is legally allowed to steal food (Hegel 1967, # 127).[34] Amartya Sen follows a similar line of argumentation when he questions the absoluteness of "the right of ownership and exchange" (Sen 1985, 5). Sen then points out that "many large famines [...] have taken place [...]without any overall decline in food availability at all, with no "natural cause" making famines inescapable. People have been deprived of food precisely because of sudden and violent shifts in "entitlements," resulting from the exercise of rights that people "legitimately" have within the given legal system" (Id.). Sen then provides a two-step argument. First, he argues that he does not see why property rules should hold when it is a matter of life and death for millions (Id., 6). Thus the government's order to the farmers to produce rice would be legitimate, even if rice is less profitable for the farmers than an alternative crop, if the order was given for the purpose of avoiding famine. Second, Sen extends this same argument to "bad-but-not-so-disastrous consequences." (Id.). Rights (property rights) so he suggests can be violated for other rights (personal liberty rights).[35]

---

[34] Hegel calls it the right of distress and points out that this idea is the basis for *beneficium competentiae*, whereby a man in debts may retain the tools of his trade. He is given the right to make a living notwithstanding the legitimate property claims of the creditor. This idea is present in US bankruptcy law where the debtor is allowed to retain up to $2,025 worth of their tools of the trade. See 11 U.S.C. § 522(d)(6).

[35] Elizabeth Anderson provides a summary of her arguments about the ethical limitations of the market when she writes: "The realization of some forms of freedom, autonomy, and welfare demands that certain goods be produced, exchanged, and enjoyed outside the market relations or in accordance with non-market norms" (Anderson, 166). Anderson, just as Hegel or Sen, does not use the concept of merit good. All three, though, provide arguments for governmental intervention in the economy on merit good grounds. Allan Buchanan too, another ethicist reflecting on the market economy, concedes that there are plausible grounds to restrict the free market without using the concept of merit good (Buchanan, 101).

Similarly, one can argue that the purpose of economic efficiency is to promote human freedom and human happiness. Once one admits this then one sees a paradox arise. The harsh rule of the free market of no free lunch is understood to be the means for creating greater freedom and happiness. That same harsh rule diminishes, however, that human freedom and happiness for some human beings. Must this harsh rule be maintained even if it undermines reaching the goal aimed at by the rule? Western societies have demonstrated that they believe that the harsh rule of the free market should be suspended for some categories of people just as property laws cease in the face of a person facing starvation or facing the impossibility of making a living. The most convincing argument has been made for the disabled. They are not able to obey the harsh rule for no fault of their own. Similar arguments are made for the unemployed, the poor and the elderly.

Again the public goods argument is insufficient to justify this existing practice. Most people are required to follow the harsh rule of the free market. Some are exempt. The cost of the exemptions is not limited to the amount people are willing to pay. Rather, the exemptions are given on the basis of ethical arguments, often beyond the level and thus the cost that consumers would pay for voluntarily. As ethical arguments have a different weight in different communities one should not be surprised that discussions about the creation of a safety net involve all kinds of value judgments.[36] Still, beyond the difference in opinions, one can conclude that Western societies have made the creation of a safety net a merit good. Here I am not discussing the disagreements about the extension of the safety network nor the methods of providing them. I limited myself to giving a philosophical argument for the provision of some safety net.

4.5.5.2 Limiting the Safety Net

Once the safety net is established the question of cost containment arises almost necessarily. The creation of a safety net goes together with the elimination of a basic rule of the free market: goods and services must be fully paid for. Indeed, with free or subsidized medical services, cost is less of a constraining factor. The consumers are not motivated as much to shop around for medications (e.g., generic drugs) as they are for market provided goods. Producers (doctors) can prescribe additional tests and increase their income without encountering resistance

---

[36] One example of the influence of value's is the way a country's religious heritage often played a role in determining how its modern welfare state developed. Catholic countries, with their emphasis on large and connected families, tend to have a smaller social welfare system in place with mechanisms that encourage the mother to stay home and care for her family. Protestant countries, with their emphasis on individualism, developed larger social welfare systems that did not place as much importance of maintaining a single-earner home. This example simply illustrates that there are different methods of providing a safety net and that some are more cost effective or more vulnerable to moral hazard than others. For additional information on religious influence on modern welfare states see Morgan and Zippel 2003; Morgan 2002; Sigrun Kahl 2005; Gill and Lundsgaarde 2004.

from the consumers. Producers (pharmaceuticals) can lobby for the government to write legislation which prohibits consumer groups (the states, which administer Medicare and Medicaid) to negotiate down the price of drugs or to allow buying the drugs cheaper across the border (say Canada). The right for need adapted education for children with learning disabilities has given rise to a group of lawyers who sue the states and the District of Columbia in order to get children with learning disabilities into expensive special education schools.

Cost containment of the safety net is mandatory as illustrated dramatically by the rapidly increasing cost of medical services. Costs for medical services have increased percentage wise more than the national product. Consequently the cost of medical services is year after year a higher percentage of the national product.

Containing costs of the safety net, particularly the medical services part, is objected to by both consumers and producers of those services. Hence, cost containment of the safety net cannot be fully defended by the public good argument. It is a merit good. If cost containment of the safety net is a very important merit good, is it not the case that CEO's of corporations providing medical service have an additional moral obligation. Could one not say that these CEO's cannot morally undertake actions that would kill the cost containment even though such cost containment is diminishing the profitability of their corporations. Such CEO's then feel the contradictory moral obligations of having both to pursue and not to pursue profitability.

4.5.6 Public Health Measures[37]

Musgrave provided early discussions of this type of merit good, by pointing out that many governments have mandatory health requirements (Musgrave 1969a, 143; Ver Eecke 2007, 32). Health has always been an issue that ties societies together. Plagues and diseases have destroyed entire cities while modern day health care costs place a burgeoning burden on all members of society. Diseases like bird flu, SARS, and the swine flu increasingly remind first world countries of their links to the third world since microscopic killers can cross borders and unite us like little else.

Health care also has a collective dimension because often the collective must pay for the effects of individual unhealthy decisions. This can partly be taken care of by the public goods idea such as the funding of research in health care up to the level for which there is a willingness to pay. But in some cases more needs to be done. To prevent infectious diseases inoculation might be enforced against the will of individuals. This demonstrates that public health policies will unavoidably also include merit good policies.

---

[37] Three of the eight "Millenium Development Goals" are connected with health issues: Goal four: Child Health. Goal 5: Maternal Health and Goal 6: Combat HIV/AIDS.

In economic terms, illness destroys human capital, therefore impairing economic growth. Diseases not only kill people but can lead to lifelong disabilities, causing a reduction in the workforce and an expense that the community must bear. Money spent on sick people will not be directed towards economic investment and development so the disease's burden on individuals and communities will last long after the illness has been effectively treated.

In ethical terms, health is a basic human good because it is essential for human freedom. Wealth, the result of economic activity is merely an instrument. Hence wealth can be used to promote health even if it is not chosen by individuals. Head's view of merit goods is here particularly relevant. He prefers to see merit goods as the government's attempt to correct distorted individual choices (Head 1966, 3–6; 1969, 215–218; 1988, 4–5; 1990, 214). Individuals often lack insight, will or proper judgment even if they do have the information.[38] When the government documents bad choices by the consumers it is uniquely capable of gathering information and creating and enforcing certain rules which promote healthy living. As these rules are imposed, sometimes against the wishes of individuals one is not in the presence of public goods, but instead one is dealing with merit goods.[39]

Let us briefly mention four subcategories of public health merit goods. The first is preventative health care measures. Examples are obligatory inoculation and the current trend to intervene in unhealthy diets.[40] The next appropriate subcategory under public health measures is governmental food and drug regulation. The third subcategory is subsidized or free pregnancy care in order to promote a healthy generation of

---

[38] Smoking provides an example of where information of health threats is widely disseminated and accepted but yet millions of people continue to smoke regardless of the ill health effects.

[39] In discussing a 2009 proposal to finance the expansion of health insurance by taxing "Cadillac insurances" (insurance plans of more than $8,500 for singles and $23,000 for families) Jonathan Gruber, a professor in economics at MIT, uses merit good arguments, not public goods arguments when he writes: "It would be progressive, in that it would take from those with the most generous insurance to finance the expansion of coverage to those without insurance" and there would be an estimated salary increase of "$223 billion over the next decade [...] 90 % would go to families with incomes below $200,000" (Gruber, A15). Note: the salary increase would be expected because employers and employees would have more incentive to use employment compensation in the form of wages rather than in taxed luxury insurance policies.

[40] Many states are enacting legislation that requires restaurants and fast food chains to post calorie and other nutrition information on their menus. Over 15 states are currently considering these measures. Kiera Manion-Fischer, "States Consider Trans Fat Bans, menu labeling" Stateline.org available at http://www.stateline.org/live/details/story?contentId=383615 (accessed Nov. 9, 2009). Massachusetts and New York are considering mandatory Body Mass Index testing for public school children, (ibid.) and Arkansas has already passed a law that requires schools to "include as part of the student report card to parents an annual body mass index percentile by age for each student." House Bill 1583; Act 1220 of 2003. New York City's ban on trans fat in all restaurants is another example of the government overriding individual consumer choice on the grounds that such action will prevent millions of dollars in health care costs. Notice of Adoption of an Amendment (§81.08) to Article 81 of the New York City Health Code (http://www.nyc.gov/html/doh/downloads/pdf/public/notice-adoption-hc-art81-08.pdf). See also (http://www.nyc.gov/html/doh/html/pr2006/pr114-06.shtml) (accessed Oct. 23, 2009).

children and to prevent, for a cohort of poor women, dangerous births. A fourth and last area of public health infrastructure is health research. It is now considered a public good but such a definition leaves it at risk for inadequate funding. With a public good, it cannot be funded past what the people would voluntary pay for and this level might not be sufficient to push for the innovations that drive health care.

4.5.7 A Well-Functioning Social Contract

It is well known that a functioning economy requires a minimal degree of peace and stability. This requires a well-functioning social contract. But generally one can say that in order to have a harmonized society that can perform economically efficiently there needs to be some kind of equality or equal opportunity so that all feel recognized, feel that they have a stake in the economy and are ready to participate in a free market.

An example of such an instance can be seen in Singapore after the country's independence. The first years of independence brought deadly riots and the government realized that something had to be done to address their cause if the country was to prosper. Their solution was twofold: a promise to more evenly distribute whatever financial successes independence brought and invest heavily in public housing and public education. The riots stopped, people began to live better and, not surprisingly, they took a greater stake in their country's economy (Ghesquiere, 48). The underpinnings of this economic success derived from the extension of equal opportunity to all, and allowing all people to feel recognized. Accepting a well-functioning social contract as a merit good allows the government to introduce some form of economic redistribution, which worked so well in Singapore (Ghesquiere, 132–33) and the other Asian Tigers during the 1990 s (Campos and Root, 1–4; 28–75; World Bank 1997, 158–167).

A well-functioning social contract has a component of a public good, but only a component. When redistribution goes beyond the wishes of some then one violates the concept of public good. It is difficult to see how a social contract including a substantial redistributive element would be without opposition. Hence an ethical argument is necessary to fully justify such a social contract. But this is a merit good justification.

4.5.8 Transparency and Prevention of Corruption

I have argued that the government has many duties with regards to the economy. When these duties involve merit goods it is the case that some people or corporations will be harmed by the exercise of the government's duties, e.g., regulations and prohibitions. One can expect that those fearing or experiencing harm will try to influence the regulatory process. There are legitimate, open and transparent ways of influencing this process. These might be deplorable as in the case of the baby food industry successfully boycotting the US health officials program to increase breast feeding.[41] There are also hidden and illegitimate forms of influencing the regulatory process in which politicians are bribed to change the outcome in favor of the briber. It is reasonable to argue that if the government has regulatory duties then measures must be taken to let the process of regulation be fair and efficient. Again, rules of transparency and prevention of corruption aim at preventing some individuals or corporations from doing what they want.[42] Consumer sovereignty is violated. Hence one is in the presence not just of a public good but of a merit good as well. That this is an important concern can be illustrated by the importance given to anti-corruption by the World Bank.[43]

4.5.9   Strategic Planning and Investment Decisions or Industrial Policy

In neo-classical economics the idea of an infant industry is so well accepted that it appears regularly in economic textbooks (Boulding 1966, 420; Samuelson 1976, 701–702, 768). The argument is made that if it is the case that increase in production diminishes the average price substantially, it might be necessary to help the beginning industry (infant industry) to grow to maturity. Contrary to Samuelson's opinion that "Probably the infant-industry argument had more validity for America a century ago than it does today" (Samuelson 1976, 702), I would like to argue that government actions were also crucial in the twentieth century for the commercialization of airplanes–the US postal service bought airplanes at a moment in time that there was no demand for airplanes– and for the start and the development of the computer industry. From a global point of view there is the success of the "Asian tigers" and there is the economic miracle of Singapore which went from underdeveloped country to developed country in 40 years. In a recent study,

---

[41] See Sect. 4.2 of this chapter.

[42] Protection against corruption requires clever regulations such as those regulating the position of the chairman of the Federal Reserve in the United States. He is appointed to a four-year term and cannot be an officer or director of any bank or hold stock in any bank or banking institution.

[43] The World Bank includes among its eleven themes two explicitly relating to our merit good category number eight. They are *Public Sector Governance* and the *Rule of Law*. Under the first we find *Other Accountability/Anti-corruption*. Under the second we find *Legal Institutions for a Market Economy*. See: http://web.worldbank.org/WBSITE/EXTERNAL/PROJECTS/0,,men uPK:51562~pagePK:64133621~piPK:64140076~theSitePK:40941,00.html, accessed August 12, 2009. Another indicator of the importance of our eight merit good category is the fact that among the publications of the World Bank there are 242 which discussion anti-corruption. See: http://books.google.com/books/worldbank?q=anti-corruption&lr=&sa=N&start=190, accessed August 12, 2009.

Ghesquiere states that: "Singapore's economic prowess over many other countries reflects superior planning and execution" (Ghesquiere, 100).

The problem of infant industry has now been generalized into the problem of industrial policy. In line with Adam Smith's idea that "By pursuing his own interest he frequently promotes that of the society more effectually than when he really intends to promote it" (Adam Smith 1937, 423), Olson develops the idea of rational ignorance when it comes to industrial policy (Olson 1986). And indeed there is a place for caution. Nelson takes another view and argues that modern capitalism is in fact a mixed economic system in that free market principles are combined with governmental regulations and decisions. The pharmaceutical industry can make profit but cannot sell many products unless they are governmentally approved. The airline industry too can try to make a profit, but it has to obey, among others, government safety guidelines. Capitalism depends upon innovation. Science is an important source of knowledge for innovation. But, so argues Nelson, corporations are not interested in funding basic research or research which is best made available to all. Such basic research has traditionally been done in universities and funded by governments (Nelson 2002).

Similarly, a study of the many publications on industrial policy provides insightful arguments for a limited industrial policy. It also shows that, in fact, all countries have consciously willed or accidentally created an industrial policy. It is our contention that conscious reflection on industrial policy is better than ad hoc improvisation. Topics mentioned in the industrial policy literature are avoidance of bottlenecks; co-ordination of production choices (Glavan; Avnimelech and Teubal; Tung and Wan); diversification (Zabortseva) and avoidance of top specialization (Brazil and coffee); promotion of entrepreneurship (Mahadea and Pillay; Dana and Galperin); proper and efficient product control (Wolfl, Wanner et al.); attracting direct foreign investment without hampering small and medium sized firms (Burke, Gorg and Hanley; Guner, Ventura and Xu); the importance of value added taxation (VAT) (de Mello); customs modernization in order to promote international trade (De Wulf and Sokol); and the more abstract discussion of neo-liberal versus neo-structuralist organization of the economy (Kirby).

The question of industrial policy is therefore not whether to have one or not, but rather the question of which industrial policies are rational (Wolnicki). In the creation of industrial policies there are losers. Hence the public argument cannot fully justify industrial policy. Merit good arguments are necessary.

4.5.10 Environmental Protection[44]

The market does not protect sufficiently against environmental harm because individual preferences (cheap but more polluting production method) that dramatically

---

[44] The seventh of the "Millenium Development Goals" is: Environmental Sustainability.

affect others (poisonous air, water or soil) are externalities that the market does not always capture, hence, their ill-effect is not captured in the price. With the expected rise of temperature the environmental problem has drastically changed. Indeed, the problem is not limited to factories using polluting production methods. Environmentalists make us aware that every consumer contributes to the pollution of the earth.

One could argue that environmental protection is justifiable as a public good. It is a matter of internalizing bad externalities. There are, however, two arguments which show that the public good argument cannot cover all aspects of environmental protection measures. First, the method used to limit industrial pollution is not the method prescribed by public good's thinking. One does not ask consumers who want less pollution, how much they are willing to pay nor does one ask the polluters how much they would have to be paid to pollute less. One does not make it a (fictitious) voluntary exchange between polluters and polluted in which one has a market kind of agreement in which every participant feels that he or she is not worse off by the new transaction (Head 1974, 152–163). Second, environmental protection imposes an immediate cost. The benefits of environmental protection come later (Broome). Human beings underestimate the value of the future (Head 1974, 219–220, with reference to the work of Pigou). Hence, the government is in a position of having to correct the consumers' evaluation of the benefits of environmental protection (Musgrave 1990, 208; Ver Eecke 2007, 62). For these two reasons, environmental protection requires also merit good arguments that justify the government's right to interfere with consumer sovereignty.

4.5.11 Protection of Cultural Heritage

This concept is not necessarily economically very important but is necessary for conceptual completion. By regulating things such as obligatory national holidays (Martin Luther King Day, the Fourth of July) and the preservation of historical sites, the government does not respect consumer sovereignty. When economic decisions are made by normative values other than the consumer preferences one is in the presence of merit good decisions (Musgrave 1990, 208; Ver Eecke 2007, 62).

The confusion between seeing the preservation and protection of historical sites as a public or a merit good is evident in court decisions about "takings" connected with historical sites. Thus in the case of Pennsylvania Central Transportation Company vs. New York City, the court imposed two burdens on Penn Central on the ground that it was a building with cultural and historical significance: "First, they were charged with keeping the exterior of the building in 'good repair;' second, they were required to seek approval for any proposed exterior architectural modifications" (Jois, 37). Penn Central claimed "that the application of the Landmarks Preservation Law had 'taken' their property without just compensation," while the Court wrote "It is, of course, true that the Landmarks Law has a more severe impact on some landowners than on others, but that in itself does not mean that the law effects a 'taking.' Legislation designed to promote the general welfare commonly burdens some more than others" (Jois 37–39). I agree with Jois's analysis, maintaining that the Court confuses the public good argument (where everybody benefits from the implementation of a public good idea (policy)) from a merit good argument (where one accepts that there are winners and losers). It is true that trucks must pay more than cars or bicycles to use a bridge financed by a toll booth, but that is because they have different benefits. Mentioning that "Penn Central owned other properties in the area that did operate at a profit" (Jois 38) is insufficient to prove that one is here in the face of a public good calculus. But accepting that the burdens imposed on Penn Central were merit good decisions might have led to the conclusion, on the basis of constitutional reasoning about property, that Penn Central needed to be compensated. Classifying a regulatory taking as a public or a merit good makes a big difference.

4.6 Applications for Business Ethics

4.6.1 General Argument

The introduction of the concept of merit good shows how ethical rules and principles can be applied in a systematic way to commercial settings, our definition of the domain of business ethics. An important part of business ethics is concerned with the internal management of corporations. But business ethicists also address questions of social responsibility of corporations. Accepting the concept of merit good will, I believe, expand the possibilities to see and discuss the social dimension in business ethics. It will also help to better understand some of the semi-hidden social dimensions of businesses that business ethicists consider. Finally, I believe that the list of merit goods has the potential to transform the treatment by business ethicists of the social dimension of the economy and thus of the environment in which businesses operate. Indeed, the concept of merit goods presents us with a list of normatively desired objectives derived from the legislative interaction of consumers as citizens such as prohibition of discrimination or the prohibition of anti-competitive practices. In the above mentioned cases the ethical demands upon business are clear and sanctioned by the law. Less clear are cases where something is already proven to be a merit good (breast-feeding) but the merit good provision is not yet law. One could argue that businesses have the ethical obligation not to stand in the way of implementing such a proven merit good. Still, as the ethical obligation is not legally sanctioned, business leaders could argue that in such cases the merit good must be weighted against their other ethical obligations. I believe that a good or service which is a proven merit good has objective validity and cannot be anymore rejected as being only the subjective expression of a na do-good attitude.[45]

Another tool to clarify the importance of the concept of merit goods for business ethics is the concept of stakeholder. The concept of stakeholder is now replacing the older notion of stockholder as the kind of person to whom the corporation is responsible.[46] The stockholders were the owners of the corporation. The stockholder view of the corporation has affinities with the emphasis of economic theory on private goods. With the concept of public goods and of externalities economic theory accepts that economic activity can have an impact on more than the owners of the goods (pollution by a factory; pollination by bees). I see an affinity between the economic concept of public goods and the concept in business ethics of stakeholder. In both, one recognizes the impact of a good or a corporation on people beyond the owners. With the introduction of the concept of merit goods, economic theory adds a new idea. The concept of public good introduced the idea that more people have an interest (a stake) in a good than the owners. The concept of merit goods argues that there are goods which are so important that people might not have a pure economic interest in a particular good or service but they have an ethical interest in that good or service (no

---

[45] Business ethicists did write about the ethical problems related to Nestlé without making use of the concept of merit good. However, looking back over the boycott of Nestlé one can, in retrospect, summarize succinctly the ethical problems related to Nestlé's business practices about handling the sales of infant formula by stating that Nestlé behaved unethically with reference to several of our series of merit goods. Nestlé's handling of infant formula created problems with reference to merit good 5 (Safety net: children are a vulnerable population), merit good 6 (public health measures); merit good 2 (Institutional arrangements to promote economic efficiency: lack of understandable information; free infant formula in hospitals which interferes with lactation of mother; pervert incentives to health workers to promote unhealthy product) and merit good 4 (Education: lack of proper information or information in appropriate language). Also fascinating is that the Philosophers Index provides the first article for a search on infant formula as the one by James C. Baker, The International Infant Formula Controversy: A Dilemma in Corporate Social Responsibility in Journal of Business Ethics 1985, Vol 4, 3, p. 181–190. Baker states that Dr. Derick Jelliffe initiated the fight against bottle feeding in 1970 (Baker, 182). The presence of merit good thinking among business ethicists might have drastically shortened the fifteen years time span between the public boycott and the first acknowledged publication in a philosophy journal about the problem. Economic journals published articles already in 1974, 1978, 1980–1981 and 1982 (Ibid. 189–190).

[46] John Hasnas on the contrary argues that the "stockholder theory is neither as outdated nor as flawed as it is sometimes made to seem"(1998, 19). Hasnas grounds his view on the principle "that a truly adequate normative theory of business ethics must ultimately be grounded in individual consent" (Ibid.). A theory of merit goods gives a place to individual consent in as much as merit good provision requires some legislative initiative. But legislation is not simply built upon individual consent alone. There is majority rule and there are constitutional rights. The theory of merit goods puts radical limits to the normative validity of the stockholder theory. The theory of merit goods can therefore be used to show an ethical problem in business practices where at least one normative theory of business ethics—stockholder theory—might not see an ethical problem for the business executives involved.

discrimination even if I am not discriminated against; breast feeding even if I am an adult male). The merit good debate can thus rightly take its place in the narrative approach to stakeholder theory (Freeman, 602) as one more background discipline providing guidance for understanding value creation in which business plays an essential role (Freeman, 604).[47] James Baker reports that in the infant formula debate there was one negative vote against the World Health Organization code: the United States (1985, 183). That vote was based on a denial of the ethical function of merit goods stressing on the contrary the idea of "a free market economic system" (Ibid.)

At the very least, the debate on merit goods will give business leaders more tools with which to make ethical and moral decisions. It will also give business leaders a greater ability to discuss government regulation. If the regulations serve the purpose of a justified merit good, business leaders would be able to see the greater rationale and purpose behind them. While they may still be an irritant to many businesses, an irritant with a strong and proven explanation would be easier to accept than an irritant with nothing supporting its rationale.[48] On the other hand, businesses would now have a new vocabulary to reject a particular law or regulation that is counter-productive or burdensome to the point that it is no longer effective. In the end, merit goods are designed to make the free market work more effectively within our social and moral boundaries.[49] With that goal clearly stated, businesses will have a much easier time accepting regulations that actually work. They will also have a way of objecting to badly conceived or badly implemented merit goods.

4.6.2 Additional Concrete Application: The Financial Crisis of 2007–2008 and the Subsequent Recession

I like to ask the following question: is there room for ethical thinking in order to provide intellectual guidelines for avoiding the repetition of the financial crisis of 2007–2008 and the subsequent recession or is it all a matter of pure economic forces. If the answer is that the disasters under discussion are purely the result of economic forces then ethics in general and business ethics in particular has little

---

[47] See how interested businesses successfully undermined the merit good program of trying to increase breast feeding (Sect. 4.2 of this chapter).

[48] Baker contrasts the more ethical handling by Johnsons & Johnson of its case of Tylenol with the more evasive and sometimes combative and misleading strategies of Nestlé in the infant formula debate.

[49] In his book, Edward Soule addresses problems not addressed in this chapter, i.e., what is the nature of good regulations. We agree with his overall point of view: "legitimate use of regulatory power over commercial activity is an ongoing and contentious work in progress" (Soule, 1). Thus simply claiming that a good is a merit good is not enough. Serious arguments must be provided and the implementation needs to be done judiciously.

or no role to play. However, if one can prove that ethical thinking can provide tools for avoiding these disasters then there is an argument for the expansion of business ethics into political economy or philosophy of economics. The theory of merit goods provides a systematic way of looking at the ethical aspects hidden in the political economic dimensions of business activity. These dimensions need not be argued anew each time or laboriously re-discovered. A review of the studies by Reinhart and Rogoff, Reich and Rajan will serve as illustration for our claim.

Reinhart and Rogoff conclude their economic analysis of the recent financial crisis and those of eight prior centuries with a hint at an ethical dimension in the financial crises they studied when they conclude their book with the following statement:

> All too often, periods of heavy borrowing can take place in a bubble and last for a surprisingly long time. But highly leveraged economies, particularly those in which continual rollover of short term debt is sustained only by confidence in relatively illiquid underlying assets, seldom survive forever, **particularly if leverage continues unchecked**. This time may seem different, but all too often a deeper look shows it is not. Encouragingly, history does point to warning signs that policy makers can look at to assess risk—if only they do not **become too drunk with their credit bubble-fueled success** (my emphasis)(292).

As if addressing the ending of the quotation by Reinhart and Rogoff, Robert Reich and Raghuram Rajan state that, once the excessive borrowing has started, it is naive to believe that policy makers will just be able to have the moral courage to reign in what they call "the financial folly." Reich and Rajan point to one of our eleven categories of merit goods as the main cause for setting the path for the financial disaster. Rajan then goes much further and uses seven of our merit good categories to explain the unfolding of the disaster, including the recession. Reich points to the fact that both the 2007–2008 and the 1929 financial crises were preceded by a decade of growing income gap between the very rich and the rest of the country which included both the middle class and the working class (Reich 20–22). Rajan stresses the fact that this occurred prior to the 2007–2008 financial crisis (Rajan 24). As a consequence people could not buy the products the economy produced. This created a situation where the American dream seemed threatened (Rajan 29–30).[50] Rajan further adds that in the US the educational system was failing. Rajan sees this as a second threat to the American dream (Rajan 24–27, 29). Education is our fourth merit good category. Reich and Rajan point out that both the Clinton and the Bush administration sensed the political danger of the waning of the American dream (Reich 51). They addressed the problem by creating cheap credit and government backing for mortgages (Rajan 35–38). One here sees that the waning of the American dream was experienced and handled as a treat to what can be called "A well functioning Social Contract," which is our

---

[50] Rajan even writes: "Without some change in this trend, destructive class warfare is no longer impossible to contemplate" (Rajan 30).

seventh merit good category.[51] The surplus of money of the very wealthy, the need of the other classes to borrow and the easing up of money provided for mortgages created the conditions for a tremendous increase in the financial sector.[52]

Three further facts made the situation of the explosion of the financial markets more dangerous. First, there was the process of deregulation of Wall Street in the previous decade (Reich 56; Rajan 33). Second, there was the refusal to regulate the new and exploding financial sector of the derivatives. This approach to the financial sector violates ideas of Adam Smith and the neo-liberals who argued that regulation of banking and credit creation is one of the three tasks necessary to create an efficient economy.[53] The idea of properly regulating the banking sector is part of our second merit good category.

Third, Rajan remarks that there was fraud in both the creation and reporting of many mortgages and that, furthermore, there was also fraud in hiding the weakness of the mortgages which were used as assets underlying the new securities that were created. Even the government was an accomplice in that HUD decided against disclosure requirements about some of these practices. (Rajan 36, 38, 127–28). Such fraud and such omission of disclosure violates merit good category eight which demands transparency and prevention of corruption.[54]

Rajan then addresses the American political situation once the financial crisis has occurred and has created a recession. First, he draws attention to two unique situations in the US compared with the rest of the industrial world. The US has a weaker safety net (merit good category five) than the rest of the Western world. Indeed, unemployment insurance is less generous and of shorter duration (Rajan 93). Furthermore, health insurance is tied to work where it is subsidized. When a worker is unemployed in the US they have to get private insurance which is more expensive than the health insurance available through the employer (Rajan 87). Health insurance becomes a heavy burden for the unemployed in the US where there was no universal health insurance until just recently. Hence there is a weak

---

[51] We find that several authors stress the importance of a "well-functioning Social Contract." Ghesquiere makes the case for the economic miracle of Singapore. Campos and Root and the World Bank 1997 make the case for the success of the Asian Tigers. Reich made the case for what he calls the Great American Prosperity from 1947 to 1975 when he writes: "the basic bargain had ensured that the pay of American workers coincided with their output. In fact, the vast middle class received an increasing share of the benefits of economic growth" (Reich 51). President Bush made an enthusiastic connection between the American dream and home owning (Rajan 37).

[52] By 2007, the financial and insurance companies accounted for more than 40 % of the American profits and almost as great a percentage of pay, up from 10 % during the great prosperity period (Reich 56–57).

[53] Besides regulations of banks and credit creation the Neo-liberals also advocated anti-trust legislation and obligatory product information (Adam Smith, 308, 313; Simons, passim).

[54] Rajan makes it clear that it is not just the corporations, which committed the fraud, which are to be blamed. Also to be blamed are the weak system of oversight created by the government and the laxity by which the existing regulations were enforced.

provision of what I classify as merit good six. The weak unemployment provisions and the problem with health insurance made the US voters very anxious. Given that each congressman or Senator in the US is a political entrepreneur, they are very sensitive to the anxieties of the electorate. Hence, they felt they had to do something quickly, much quicker than, for instance, Europe. Therefore, dealing with the recession occurred under a double burden; First, the stimulus package had to be done quickly. What is done quickly is often not done efficiently. Also, the stimulus package was used to finance many pet projects which could not be considered effective Keynesian medicine, such as money for cancer research (Rajan 99; Drew 2).

Second, in order to be effective the American stimulus package also needed to stimulate the rest of the world, given that the US is also importantly an importer of foreign goods and given that other countries could wait given that they had better unemployment benefits and health insurance in place (Rajan 100). Hence the US faced unique problems in dealing with the third category of merit goods: the business cycle. When the economic recovery faltered in 2011 one saw further weaknesses emerge in the ability of the US political system to manage the business cycle. In the boom years the US had not paid back its debt. This made it more difficult to use Keynesian policies to overcome the looming recession.[55]

Even though the American political system is responsible for making the recent recession more punitive than it should have been, it remains true that the real cause is the crisis in the financial system. I now want to return to that crisis.

Rajan argues that people in the financial sector knew of the potential disaster created by the risks involved in the creation of securities. These risks received the name of tail risk (Rajan 136–137). First, there were people who knew about that risk but they had no decision power even though they were active players in the game. These people knew because they saw that the system "paid hefty bonuses when employees made profits but did not penalize them significantly when they incurred losses" (Rajan 139). It was so well known to these people that they created names for this potential risk such as the Acapulco Play, IBG (I'll be gone if it doesn't work), and in Chicago, the O'Hare Option (buy a ticket departing from O'Hare International Airport: if the strategy fails, use it; it the strategy succeeds, tear up the ticket and return to the office (Ibid.)).

Second, there were people who knew about this risk and had the power to take action. Some did take action. Most did not. One that did was Jamie Dimon, CEO of JP Morgan. He had two ideas and made an important decision. His first idea

---

[55] Reinhart & Rogoff, Reich and Rajan all studied the financial crisis. Only Rajan presents an overall view. All three show their excitement in discovering causes and connections. It looks as if they have to invent these causes and connections. The availability of a list of merit goods might make the search for causes and connections easier. Consideration of the full list of merit goods in understanding an economic disaster might become the norm for the completeness of the study. The completeness of this study by Rajan might be one of the reasons for the great regard Rajan continues to hold in the economic profession (The Economist, Feb 10, 2011).

was that if he did not understand how a business made money he would decide to not participate in it. His second idea was that there are business cycles and you can assume that every 5 years something bad can happen. Hence, he argued forcefully that it was necessary to build a "fortress balance sheet." (Rajan 143–144). Dimon also made an important decision to help to translate his insights into pragmatic decision making. Dimon increased the pay for risk analysts so that he could attract the best people and so that the risk analysis department would have clout. Other CEOs made the opposite decision. They paid risk analysts and managers substantially less than those in operational units who created the risky but profitable financial instruments. They also fired courageous and foresighted risk analysts such as Richard Fuld from Lehman did with Mike Gelband (Rajan 140, 145).

It is also worth taking a look at the CEOs who did not take action in the face of known risks. Rajan reports that some did not understand. Some did understand the potential risk and took no action because any reasonable action in the face of known risk would have to curtail the options for the brilliant and aggressive group of creators of financial instruments.

Citigroup's CEO, Chuck Prince, for instance, figured that such action would lead him to lose these brilliant people and in turn this would diminish the competitiveness of that important division of his Citigroup (Rajan 143).

Rajan also presents two reasons for not acting which have obvious ethical implications. The first such reason is the fact of limited liability which is included in our first merit good category. The creators of financial instruments with limited liability were sure that they could benefit from the gains of their risk taking whereas they were sure they would not be obliged to pay for the enormous losses if they were to occur. The question then arises: who would bear the losses of the risk-taking if something bad were to happen. This leads us to the second reason why some CEOs did not act. The mortgage backed securities were highly diversified. A serious crisis could happen only if mortgages across the country were to default. It could not happen if only here and there pockets of default occurred. But the leaders of the financial industry figured out that if there was a country wide reason for substantial mortgage failures then the government would have to step in. They figured that the government would not be able to tolerate a massive country wide mortgage failure (Rajan 148). They also figured that if the massive country wide mortgage failure could not be stopped it would lead to a liquidity crisis for all the major banks. This in turn would lead to difficulties in borrowing by small and large businesses and would lead to a catastrophic decrease of economic activity. The CEOs of the big financial institutions figured that the government would not let that happen and that they would be bailed out (Rajan 149). Singularly or jointly they were too important to fail. Rajan documents the different actions the government did take when the crisis occurred (Rajan 149–152).

Clearly, Adam Smith's idea of the market failed. Adam Smith argues that if individual actors are able to profit from their actions but are also made to pay for the negative consequences of their actions then society as a whole necessarily benefits (Adam Smith, 421, 423). In the analysis of the financial crisis one learns that it was not the case that individual actors were forced to pay for the bad consequences of their actions. Business ethicists can agree that the economic system should not allow for a situation in which massive profits can be made by a method which risks the collapse of the whole economic system. I have shown that crucial actors knew they were walking such a path. One can also see that simple moral exhortation is useless. Hence, I argue that business ethicists, in order to be effective in helping to prevent immoral economic decision processes at the highest level of economic power, need to study how to prevent such disastrous opportunities. It is our conviction that this requires nothing less than understanding political economy. And I have shown that understanding the eleven categories of merit goods provides both a handy list of tasks one can expect that the government must take responsibility for and a compelling argument that business ethicists cannot exclude political economic considerations if they wish their moral reflections to be complete. I agree that the government might take irresponsible actions in these different domains, but not taking any action is equally irresponsible. In order to deal with the immoral dimensions of the decision making process at the highest level of economic activity business ethicists will need also to do philosophy of economics.

4.6.3 Conclusion

Our defense of eleven categories of merit goods has created a broad schema of areas in which I believe government must interfere to make the economy work and work efficiently and justly. However, I have not decided the amount of resources that should be allocated in the above areas, how such decisions should be made nor have I addressed how far each category should reach. It is our opinion that disagreements are possible, and likely, on how to formulate the institutional arrangements and the regulations to deal with these eleven areas. However, lively debate should not nullify the overall conclusion that in these areas the government can legitimately make merit good decisions. Conservatives, libertarians, socialists, feminists, and Christian democrats will all have different views of the role of the state in these different domains. This shows how philosophy will unavoidably be involved in the formulation of merit good policies.

References

Anderson E (1993) Value in ethics and economics. Harvard University Press, Cambridge

Avnimelech G, et al (2004) Strength of market forces and the successful emergence of Israel's venture capital industry: insights from a policy-led case of structural change. Revue Economique 55(6):1265–1300

Baker JC (1985) The International infant formula controversy: a dilemma in corporate social responsibility. J Bus Ethics 4(3):181–190

Boulding KE (1966) Economic analysis vol I microeconomics. Harper & Row, New York

Brennan G, Lomasky L (1983) Institutional aspects of 'Merit Goods' analysis. Finanzarchiv, N.F. 41:183–206

Brennan G, Lomasky L (1993) Paternalism, self-paternalism, and the state. In: Democracy and decision: the pure theory of electoral preference. Cambridge University Press, Cambridge pp 143–166

Buchanan A (1985) Ethics, efficiency, and the market. Rowman & Allanheld, Totowa

Burke A, et al (2008) The Impact of foreign direct investment on new firm survival in the UK: evidence for static versus dynamic industries. Small Bus Econ 31(4):395–407

Burrows P (1977) 'Efficient' pricing and government interference. In: Michael P (ed.) Public expenditure: allocation between competing ends. Cambridge University Press, Cambridge, pp 81–93

Campos JE, Root H (1996) The key to the asian miracle. Brookings Institute, Washington

Dana LP, Galperin Bella (2008) The role of government policy in post-communist Europe: a multi-country qualitative study. Glob Bus Econ Rev 106(4):467–490

de Mello L (2008) The Brazilian "Tax War": the case of value-added tax competition among states. Public Finan Rev 36(260):169–193

De Wulf L, Sokol JB (2005) Customs modernization handbook. The World Bank, Washington

Freeman RE (1997) The Blackwell encyclopedic dictionary of business ethics. Blackwell Business, Cambridge, pp 602–606

Friedman M (1953) Essays in positive economics. University of Chicago Press, Chicago

Ghesquiere H (2007) Singapore's success. Engineering economic growth. Thomson, Singapore

Gill A, Lundsgaarde E (2004) State welfare spending and religiosity: a cross-national analysis. Ration Soc 16(4):399–436

Glavan B (2008) Coordination economics, poverty traps, and the market process: a new case for industrial policy?' Indep Rev 13(260):225–243

Guner N, et al (2008) Macroeconomic implications of size-dependent policies. Rev Econ Dyn 112(4):721–744

Hasnas J (1998) The normative theories of business ethics: a guide for the perplexed. Bus Ethics Q 19:19–42

Head JG (1966) On merit goods. Finanzarchiv, N.F. 25(1):1–29 (Also published in Head, John. Public Goods and Public Welfare 1974, 214–247)

Head JG (1969), `Merit Goods Revisited,' *Finanzarchiv, N.F.*   vol. 28, No. 2, March, pp. 214–225, Also published in Head, John. Public Goods and Public Welfare. 1974, 248-261

Head JG (1974) Public goods and public welfare. Duke University Press, Durham

Head JG (1988) On merit wants: reflections on the evolution, normative status and policy relevance of a controversial public finance concept. Finanzarchiv, N.F. 46:1–37 (Also published in Rationality, Individualism and Public Policy. Geoffrey Brennan and Cliff Walsh, Eds. Canberra: Australian National University, 1990, 211–244)

Head JG (1990) On merit wants: reflections on the evolution, normative status and policy relevance of a controversial public finance concept. In: Geoffrey B, Cliff W (eds.) Rationality, individualism and public policy. The Australian National University, Canberra, pp 210–244

Head JG (2008) Review of: Wilfried Ver Eecke, an anthology regarding merit goods. West Lafayette. Purdue University Press, Indiana 2007. http://www.amazon.com/Anthology-Regarding-Merit-Goods-Unfinished/dp/1557534284/ref=sr_1_3?s=books&ie=UTF8&qid=1343652299&sr=1-3&keywords=Ver+Eecke

Hegel GWF (1967) Hegel's philosophy of right (Knox. T. M., Trans.) Oxford University Press, Oxford

Henningsen K (2007) A Great econ book for any discipline. http://www.amazon.com/Anthology-Regarding-Merit-Goods-Unfinished/dp/1557534284/ref=sr_1_3?s=books&ie=UTF8&qid=1343652299&sr=1-3&keywords=Ver+Eecke

Jois GU (2006) Can't touch this! private property, takings, and the merit goods argument. South Tex Law Rev, Vol. 48, No. 1, pp. 183-257

Kahl S (2005) The religious roots of modern poverty policy: Catholic, Lutheran and Reformed Protestant traditions compared. Eur J Soc 46:91–126

Kant I (1956) Critique of practical reason (Lewis White Beck, Trans.). The Bobbs-Merrill Company, Indianapolis

Kaufman M, et al (2007) HHS toned down breast-feeding ads. Formula industry urged softer campaign. Washington Post, 31 August, p A1 and A4

Keynes JM (1965) The general theory of employment, interest, and money. Harcourt, Brace & World, Inc., New York

Kirby P (2009) Neo-structuralism and reforming the Latin American state: lessons from the Irish case. Econ Soc 38(12):132–153

Mahadea D, et al (2008) Environmental conditions for SMME development in a South African province. S Af J Econ Manag Sci 11(4):431–448

Manion-Fisher K (2009 Assessed, 9 November) States consider Trans fat bans, menu Labeling. Accessed 09 Nov 2009

McLure CE (1968) Merit wants: a normative empty box. Finanzarchiv, N.F. 27(2):474–483

Morgan KJ (2002) Forging the frontiers between church, state, and family: religious cleavages and the origins of early childhood education in France, Sweden, and Germany. Politics and Society

Morgan KJ, Zippel K (2003) Paid to care: the origins and effects of care leave policies in Western Europe. Soc Politics 10(1):49–85

Musgrave RA (1956) A multiple theory of budget determination. Finanzarchiv, N.F. 17(3):333–343

Musgrave RA (1959a) The theory of public finance, Musgrave at Michigan University. McGraw-Hill Book Company, New York

Musgrave RA (1969a) Provision for social goods. In: Margolis J, Guitton H (eds.) Public Economics. Macmillan Press Ltd, London

Musgrave RA (1971) Provision for social goods in the market system. Public Finance 26:304–320

Musgrave RA (1990) Merit goods. In: Geoffrey B, Cliff W (eds.) Rationality, individualism and public policy. The Australian National University, Canberra, pp 207–210

Musgrave RA, Musgrave P (1973) Public finance in theory and practice. McGraw-Hilll Book Company, First Edition, New York

Nawroth EE (1961) Die Sozial- und Wirtschaftsphilosophie Des Neoliberalismus. F. H. Kerle Verlag, Heidelberg

Nelson RR (2002) The problem of market bias in modern capitalist economies. Ind Corpor Change 11(2):207–244

Oakeshott I (2009 Assessed, 9 November) Hewitt: smokers should stop before they're treated. Accessed 09 Nov 2009

Olson M, Jr (1968) Economics, sociology, and the best of all possible worlds. Public Int 12:96–118

Olson M, Jr (1986) Supply-Side economics, industrial policy, and rational ignorance. In: Claude EB, William AS (eds.) The politics of industrial policy. American Enterprise Institute for Public Policy Research, Washington, pp 245–269

Rajan RG (2010) Fault lines. How hidden fractures still threaten the world economy Princeton University Press, Princeton

Reich RB (2010) Aftershock. The next economy and America's fure. Alfred A. Knopf, New York

Reinhart CM, Rogoff KS (2009) This time it is different: eight centuries of financial folly. Princeton University Press, New Jersey

Rushe D (2012) Jamie dimon defends jp morgan in testy house committee hearing. The Guardian, New York

Samuelson PA (1954) The pure theory of public expenditure. Rev Econ Stat 36:387–389

Samuelson PA (1967) Economics. 7th edn. McGraw-Hill, Inc., New York

Samuelson PA, Temin P (1976) Economics. McGraw-Hill Book Company, New York

Scheer C (1975) Sozialstaat und Öffentliche Finanzen. Peter Hanstein Verlag GmbH, Köln

Schmidtz D (1991) The limits of government: an essay on the public goods argument. Westview Press, Boulder

Schumpeter (2010) Making a success of failure. America's enlightened treatment of bankrupt Firms remains a model to the world. The Economist, January.

Simons HC (1948) Economic policy for a free society. University of Chicago Press, Chicago

Smith A(1937) The wealth of nations. The Modern Library, New York

Soule E (2002) Morality markets. The ethics of government regulation. Rowman & Littlefield Publishers, Inc., Lanham

Steinhauer J (2008) California bars restaurant use of trans fats. New York Times, pp (A1)

Stiglitz JE (1999) Whither reform? Ten years of the transition. World Bank, WEB, pp 1–32

Stretton H, Orchard L (1994) Public goods, public enterprise, public choice: theoretical foundations of the contemporary attack on government. St. Martin's Press, New York

Sunstein C, Thaler (2003) Liberal paternalism is not an oxymoron. Univ Chic Law Rev 70:1159–1202

Tung A, et al (2007) Co-evolution of the electronics industry: policy interactions across the pacific. Pac Econ Rev 12(4):445–465

Ver Eecke W (1983) Ethics in economics: from classical economics to neo-liberalism. Philos Soc Crit 9:145–168

Ver Eecke W (2007) An anthology regarding merit goods. The unfinished ethical revolution in economic thought. Purdue University Press, West Lafayette

Ver Eecke W (2008) Ethical dimensions of the economy. Making use of hegel and the concepts of public and merit goods. Springer, Berlin

Wildavsky A (1987) Opportunity costs and merit wants. In: Speaking truth to power: the art and craft of policy analysis, chapter 7. Transaction Publishers; Previously, Little, Brown and Company, Somerset

Will GF (2012) Break up the banks. In: The Washington Post, October 14, p A21

Wolfl A, et al (2009) Ten years product market reform in OECD countries: insight from a revised PMR indicator. In: Economics department working papers: 695. OECD

Wolnicki M (2009) The post-conservative orphan: why the USA needs and effective government economic policy. Intern J Soc Eco 36(1–2):2–22

World Bank (1997) World development report 1997: the state in a changing world. Oxford University Press, New York

Zabortseva YN (2009) A structural approach to diversification of the emerging economy of kazakhstan. Intern J Econ Policy Emerg Econ 29(12):23–40

Chapter 5
The Ethical and Socio-Political Dimensions of the Financial Crisis of 2007–2008 and the Subsequent Recession

Abstract In this chapter I make use of the publications of Reinhart and Rogoff, Reich and Rajan to understand the causes of the financial crisis of 2007–2008 and the ensuing recession. Reich and Rajan go beyond a purely economic analysis and introduce socio-political factors such as the income gap between the very rich and the rest of society in the decade before the crisis, the lack of regulations of the financial sector, the use of easy mortgages to keep the American dream alive, and the fraudulent treatment of some mortgages and the derivatives based on them. These socio-political factors touch upon ethical problems. The ethical dimension in economic thinking has been captured by Musgrave's concept of merit goods. Reich and Rajan make use of seven of my eleven categories of merit goods to explain both the financial crisis of 2007–2008 and the characteristics of the ensuing recession. I end the chapter by showing that the American political system is currently not capable of delivering the merit good decisions required for dealing in a reasonable way with the challenges that led to the financial crisis and the recession caused by it.

Keywords Financial crisis • Income gap • Socio-political factors • American dream • Regulations • Recession • Business cycle • Capitalism • Merit goods • Public goods • Debt • Education • Safety net • Health insurance • Tail risk • Unemployment • Cheap money • Ethical

5.1 Introduction

I will start by summarizing the views of Keynes on recessions and of Schumpeter on economic growth. I will then point out that recently some economists have taken a socio-political perspective in looking for causes for the financial crisis and the handling of the recession which followed the financial crisis. Such a socio-political perspective introduces an ethical dimension in economic thinking. I then connect that ethical dimension of economic thinking to Musgrave's ethical economic concept of merit goods and my own creation of merit good categories. Next, I contrast the Reinhart/Rogoff view of the financial crisis with the one developed by Reich/Rajan. In my conclusion I then show how the Reich/Rajan approach makes use of seven of my eleven merit good categories to clarify the 2007–2008 financial crisis and the subsequent recession. In doing so I am able to highlight the ethical dimension in the Reich/Rajan analysis of the recent financial crisis and the recession it caused.

5.2 Keynes on Recessions and Schumpeter on Creative Destruction

Both Keynes and Schumpeter demonstrate that the economy does not develop smoothly over time. Keynes points to the painful event of recessions and Schumpeter points to the painful aspects of economic growth in which innovation makes older production methods obsolete and thus has bankruptcies as a foreseeable consequence. The ideas of these two authors suggest a similar question: can the pain connected with economic activity over time be diminished? Is this a worthwhile goal? Who is responsible for diminishing this unavoidable pain? Can the economic actors of the free market system alone achieve this goal or do we need also to rely on the government and the political process? In other words, can economic theory avoid becoming political economy?

The economy has cycles. There are booms and there are recessions-even depressions. In recessions there is less demand, hence factories do not get as many orders.[1] In order to deal with such a diminished demand factory owners and managers diminish production, cut costs and/or go bankrupt. Less production leads to less demand for work and hence increased unemployment. The recession/depression part of the economic cycle is painful.

Keynes understood recessions/depressions as directly related to a lack of demand (Keynes 23–34). Hence, Keynes recommended that the lack of demand be corrected by the only agent capable of doing so: the government. Keynes hereby gave the government a constructive task in managing the pains connected with the business cycle. In the past, governments have used two approaches to increase demand; Governments have increased spending or they have decreased taxes with the idea that such a measure increases spending power of the people. Each of these approaches requires legislative action. Such legislative action is often slow and late. Most countries have a way to increase spending automatically when recession/depression hits the population by way of increased unemployment insurance payments. Indeed, many countries provide automatically substantial unemployment benefits. Hence, many countries have a partial remedy against recessions/

---

[1] Keynes attributed the lack of demand to the degree and the slowness of the adjustment of prices and wages in a downturn of the economy.

depressions.[2] This partial remedy, however, needs to be complemented by specific Keynesian inspired legislative actions either in the form of investment or in the form of tax cuts.

Schumpeter presented a totally different view of the painful aspects inherent in a competitive economy. For Schumpeter, the capitalist system is a competitive system where the death (bankruptcy) of inefficient factories is the opportunity for the development of a more efficient economy. The capitalist system is built with creative destruction (Schumpeter 216 and 245). Stiglitz has criticized the automatic application of Schumpeter's thought. Stiglitz has argued that Schumpeter's thought requires that the system be able to incorporate the productive resources of the dying (bankrupt) factories quickly and efficiently. The system needs to find work for the workers that were let go and find new usage for the buildings and other tangible assets of the bankrupt factories. Stiglitz argued that Schumpeter's idea was misapplied in several cases after the withdrawal and the fall of the Soviet Union. Stiglitz argued that one should not let marginally inefficient factories go bankrupt if there are not available other efficient factories nor a judiciary system which can promote the absorption of the productive resources from the inefficient factories (Stiglitz, 5–8).

5.3 Recent Economic Thoughts About Financial Crises and Recessions

With the advent of the current financial crisis and the subsequent recession new thoughts have emerged. Several authors have argued that the financial crisis and the subsequent recession were endogenously engineered. The arguments developed make use of socio-economic ideas which reach beyond the strict neo-classical economic model. Briefly, the arguments advanced are that an increase in income and wealth disparity leads to a change in the financial world. The reason is that the super-rich have more funds by which they can speculate or provide loans to the less well off in society. The equilibrium requires that the less well off borrow more and thus accumulate more debt. Under these circumstances the financial sector explodes. New financial instruments are created without enough protection against bad times. The increase in debt by the less well off increases the potential for more bankruptcies. These facts make a financial crisis highly likely. The financial crisis in turn creates a recession. The reaction to this recession is partially dictated by the existence of the quality of the safety net, the availability of health insurance and the feelings about the experience of the social contract. The weakness of the safety net and the absence of universal health insurance in the US and hence the

---

[2] On the tax side there are also automatic stabilizers. First, progressive taxation means that lower economic activity in depression means that lower tax rates apply. Second, the total tax bill for the country is tied to the level of GDP.

experienced threat to the American dream put strong pressure on the American political system.[3] Pressure for quick action almost guaranteed that the stimulus package would include some inefficient items. This narrative about the 2007–2008 financial crisis and its subsequent recession demand that we do not just make an economic analysis but that we do a socio-political analysis as well. This in turn reveals ethical dimensions in the economy.

5.4 Introduction of an Ethical Concept in Economic Theory

Let us here briefly summarize the essential ideas which we developed in Chap. 3. Richard Musgrave introduced a new concept to think systematically about the socio-political dimension of the economy as it includes ethical elements. Since Adam Smith, the concept of private good has had a normative function in economic thinking. Adam Smith situated human beings as competitors for both the consumption and production of such private goods, be they apples, oranges or spades and desks (Smith, 651). However, the economics profession discovered that several goods have unusual characteristics such as non-rivalness in consumption (sometimes also called a multiple user good) and non-exclusion possibility (the good can be enjoyed without first paying for it) (Ver Eecke 2008, 134). If we take the example of a street light we notice that if one family buys and installs a street light other people can enjoy the safety provided by the light without the buyer feeling any loss in his/her own enjoyment. The good can thus be enjoyed by many at the same time. This is clearly different from, say an apple, which can only be eaten by one. The street light, this new kind of economic good, has one more characteristic. The buyer cannot exclude other people from enjoying, say, the safety of the street light. Hence, there is no possibility to exclude other people until they pay. Hence, for such goods payment is a challenge. Such a good is named a public good. Samuelson and Olson provided different approaches on how to deal with the payment problem and thus to create the ability to provide the opportunity for gain for the group of people interested in the good (Ver Eecke 2008, 135–144). One crucial idea present in thinking about private goods remains in the thinking about public goods: i.e., ideally nobody should be worse off by the provision of the public good and the good must be paid for by the ones consuming the public good. At least in theory, the idea of a free contract is still maintained.

Musgrave then presents a number of economic events which do not fit the definition of either private or public good. He names "publicly furnished school lunches, subsidized low-cost housing, and free education" (Musgrave 1959a, 13;

---

[3] Some authors include universal health insurance in the idea of a safety net. I make a separate category of universal health insurance.

Ver Eecke 2007, 24–25) or liquor on which a penalty tax (sometimes also called sin tax) is imposed (Ibid.). For those goods Musgrave created the name of merit or demerit goods. They are goods which are so meritorious or so demeritorious that the government is correct in deciding that too much (demerit good such as liquor) or too little (merit good such as education, low-cost housing and subsidized lunches for poor children) is consumed. Hence the government can interfere with the wishes of the consumers so as to make them consume more or less than they would do on their own volition. Different authors have developed different justifications for the government's intervention with consumer sovereignty (Ver Eecke 2007, 8 and 238–319). In my approach I articulated eleven domains in which the government needs to make decisions in which at least some consumers' sovereignty is not respected.[4] In articulating eleven domains for the idea of merit goods I go beyond Musgrave.[5] It is intellectually fascinating to notice that in recent reflections about the financial crisis and the subsequent recession economists make use of seven of my merit good categories to explain these troubling recent economic events.[6] Indeed, the explanations of at least Reich and Rajan do not restrict themselves to strictly economic arguments in the narrow sense. They make use of socio-political arguments as well. Both also stress the ethical aspect of their socio-political argumentation. But not all economists go that route.

5.5 Financial Crises in the Past

There are at least two different interpretations of the recent financial crisis of 2007–2008. One, presented by Reinhart and Rogoff, argues that financial crises have been around for a long time. There have been many causes and we can expect such crises to reappear again. The other, presented by Rajan and Reich, argues that the 2007–2008 financial crisis has lots of similarity with the 1929 crisis. This latter

---

[4] The list of domains in which I argue the government has to make merit good kind of decisions is the following: (1) Defining and protecting property rights including granting limited liability. (2) Institutional arrangements to promote economic efficiency including banking regulations. (3) Dealing with business cycles. (4) Education. (5) Safety net. (6) Public health measures. (7) A well-functioning social contract. (8) Transparency and prevention of corruption. (9) Strategic planning and investment decisions or industrial policy. (10) Environmental protection. (11) Protection of cultural heritage (Chap. 3).

[5] "it is clear that Ver Eecke regards the merit goods concept as having much wider application than Musgrave himself has ever suggested. He argues this very persuasively on a case-by-case basis in summarising the contributions from a wider literature in Part III of the volume (Ver Eecke 2007). With this view, I would emphatically concur" (Head 2008).

[6] The categories used by different authors are: breakdown of a well-functioning social contract (gap in income distribution threatened American dream); a weak safety net; absence of universal health insurance; failing education system; lack of transparency; lack of banking regulations and responsibility for turning around a recession (responsibility for avoiding the pains of the business cycle).

interpretation sees in the emergence of greater inequality in incomes one of the causes of the latest financial crises and thus suggest that such financial crises can be avoided.[7] Moral arguments are central in this second view. I will organize the moral arguments of this second interpretation by means of the moral concept in economics of merit goods and of merit goods categories.

5.5.1 Reinhart and Rogoff's Interpretation

I will start by presenting the view of Reinhart and Rogoff. We get a hint at the main thesis of the authors if we understand the title of their book ironically: *This Time is Different. Eight Centuries of Financial Folly.* Indeed, in their conclusion the authors quote approvingly the title of the first chapter of Kindleberger's classic book: *Manias, Panics and Crashes: A History of Financial Crises,* i.e., "Financial Crisis: A Hardy Perennial" (Reinhart and Rogoff 2009, 292).[8] Hence, the view of Reinhart and Rogoff is that the reaction of shock and dismay at the financial crisis of 2007–2008 is unjustified. For these two authors, financial crises are a re-occurring part of our economic history. Reinhart and Rogoff do take a broader view of financial crises than Rajan and Reich do. They count five forms of financial crises: external debt default, domestic debt default, banking crisis, currency crashes and inflation outbursts.

The authors state that all emerging markets go through bouts of high inflation (Reinhart and Rogoff 2009, 180). Taking a grand view the authors show in Fig. 12 (Reinhardt and Rogoff 2008, 41; Also 2009, 178 here labeled Fig. 11.2) that from 1400 until 1850 the average silver content of money in Europe diminished from 8.5 g in 1400 in the currency to 1 g in 1850. In Tables 11 through 13 the authors illustrate how many years inflation was above 20 % and above 40 %. They also list the maximum annual inflation for different countries. Since 1800 seven countries have had inflation exceeding 10,000 % (Reinhart and Rogoff 2009, 186).

Reinhart and Rogoff also deny that financial crises are less likely now because of the claim that now governments rely more on domestic debt. The authors demonstrate in Fig. 10 (Reinhart and Rogoff 2008, 38; 2009, 123 here labeled Fig. 8.4 and for the years 1827–2003) that between 1800 and 2006 there was already a joint increase of both external and domestic debt. Hence, the observation that now governments rely more on domestic debt is not sustainable and furthermore not a guarantee that financial crises will not occur again. Actually, domestic debt had an impact on external defaults.

About banking crises called crises at a financial center the authors analyze three cases: London 1825–1826; German and Austrian stock market collapse May 1873 and the Baring crisis in 1890. They point out that the causes and the outcomes are different in each case. The London crisis started by a default of Peru which scared

---

[7] For a recent publication on the negative consequences of inequality see: Stiglitz. *The Price of Inequality.*

[8] See also their paper (2008), 53.

the bond holders in London about all Latin American bonds. As a consequence bond prices of South American countries collapsed (Reinhart and Rogoff 2008, 35). The German and Austrian stock market collapse was caused by speculation in both Germany and Austria as a consequence of the indemnity paid by France to Prussia in 1871 (Ibid). The consequences spread to the whole of Europe, even to the Ottoman Empire and Latin America. The Baring crisis on the other hand only led to the insolvency of the House of Barings, the major lender to Argentina which stopped payment of dividends. A reader gets the impression that financial banking crises occur regularly, they occur for different reasons and they have different results.

Reinhardt and Rogoff document in Figs. 1 through 3 that "waves of increased capital mobility are often followed by a string of domestic banking crises" (Reinhart and Rogoff 2008, 4–8; also Reinhart and Rogoff 2009, 156 labeled Fig. 10.1). The authors point out that in emerging markets which often export raw materials we see a cycle of prosperity leading to "a ramp-up of borrowing that collapses into default when prices [of the raw materials] drop." (Reinhart and Rogoff 2008, 31–32; 2009, 77–78).

Reinhardt and Rogoff make one very important observation: "It is notable that the non-defaulters, by and large, are all hugely successful growth stories" (Reinhart and Rogoff 2008, 15; Reinhart and Rogoff 2009, 44). The authors caution against using the potential moral argument that avoiding default is economically efficient. Instead they confess that they do not know whether "high growth rates help avert default, or [if] averting default beget[s] high growth rates" (Reinhart and Rogoff 2008, Ibid).

Reinhart and Rogoff provide a wealth of data on five kinds of financial crises. They demonstrate that all kinds have occurred regularly in the past. They have pointed to different reasons for these crises and have also pointed to very different outcomes of different crises. It is true that the authors also pointed to many common features in financial crises which can be captured by the use of indicators and signals. Their main message, as I see it though, is that the claim that the world has learned from past financial crises is wrong. Their implicit message is that financial crises are here to stay because policy makers have not learned from the past and hence will repeat the same mistakes (Also Strauss-Kahn, 5–6)

One optimistic observation made by the authors is that countries which avoid one kind of financial crisis, i.e., defaults are models of economic growth. However, they confess not to have an insight of the causal relationship between lack of default and economic growth. Still, we see here the possible coincidence rather than the opposition between a morally desirable goal (no defaults) and economic efficiency (growth).

5.5.2 Rajan and Reich's Interpretation

Let us now turn to two authors who see the latest financial crisis in a different light. Both Raghuram Rajan and Robert Reich introduce also socio-political factors in their analysis of the 2007–2008 financial crisis. Reich, more than Rajan, sees a parallelism between the events preceding the 1929 and the 2007–2008 financial crash and the depression or recession that followed.

Reich sees three parallelisms. He argues that in both cases the financial crash was preceded by a growing income gap between the very rich and the rest of the country which includes both the middle class and the working class (Reich 22). In both cases the middle class and the lower class could afford financing the rising living standards, made possible by the increase in the nation's output and the production of new things, only by saving less or going into debt (Reich 23). Finally, in both cases the very wealthy used their new income to speculate on a limited range of assets (Ibid).

Let us take a closer look at the three parallelisms. I will borrow arguments from both authors. First, there is the claim of a growing income gap between the very rich and the rest of society. First, there is the period before 2008. In 1975 the 90th percentile earner had an income which was three times greater than the 10th percentile earner. By 2005 the 90th percentile earner earned five times more (Rajan 24).[9] Second, there is the similarity between the period before 1929 and 2008 as measured by the share of the nation's wealth obtained by the richest 1 % or the richest one tenth of 1 %. The share of total income going to the richest 1 percent of Americans peaked in both 1928 and 2007 at more than 23 % (Reich 20–21). The same pattern held true for the highest one tenth of 1 % whose income peaked in the same 2 years at more than 11 %. Between these two peaks there was a slow decrease of the gap between the rich and the rest of society where the one percent richest people saw their share diminish from 23 % to 9 % in the early 1970's. Thereafter the share of the rich again increased until it reached again 23 % in 2007 (Reich ibid.).[10]

The second phenomenon is that both the lower and the middle class diminished their savings and/or increased their debt. "Total mortgage debt was almost three times higher in 1929 than in 1920" (Reich 23). Household debt, including mortgage "rose from 55 % of household income in the 1960s to […] 138 % in 2007" (Reich 23).

The third parallel is that both the 1929 depression and the 2008 recession were preceded by speculation financed by money of the rich and debts by the middle class.[11] "The Dow Jones Stock Index ballooned from 63.9 in mid-1921 to a peak of 381.2 eight years later" (Reich 24). "The Dow Jones Industrial Average reached eight thousand on July 16,1997 and eleven thousand on May 3, 1999.[…] The Dow dropped when these bubbles burst (dot-com and fiber-optic cable) but recovered […]rising to twelve thousand on October 19, 2006, then to thirteen thousand on April 25, 2007" (Reich 24).

---

[9] 90th percentile earner means a person earning more than 90 % of the population.

[10] The above facts are also documented in Kumhoff and Rancière 6–8.

[11] "the earnings of corporate employees in the financial sector relative to employees in other sectors started climbing around 1980, as the sector was deregulated" (Rajan 142).

Both Reich and Rajan see in the growing gap in income by the very rich and the rest of society and the ill considered response to it as an important cause for the financial crises of 1929 and 2007–2008 which then led to a depression or a recession. Rajan adds additional socio-political dimensions to his reasoning. He argues that in America there is an absence of jealousy of the rich, among others, because of the so-called American dream based on Horatio Alger stories and the belief that the poor can become rich (Rajan 29–30). Rajan argues that by 2000 the belief in that American dream became threatened.[12] I see two important facts contributing to the threat of the American dream, even though Rajan sees them as linked together. The first fact threatening the American dream was the experience of a steadily growing income gap. The second fact starting to undermine the American dream was the failure of the American education system.

Rajan tells a rich story. First, he points out that the very rich are not so much the hereditary rich any more as they are the working rich, the ones who worked themselves up such as Bill Gates or Lloyd Blankfein (head of Goldman Sachs). Actually, at the end of the twentieth century 80 % of the income of the richest 0.01 % of Americans comes from wages and income from self owned businesses (Rajan 25–26). Hence, it is human Capital which provides the path towards the American dream. And this is true not just for the very rich but for everybody as can be seen by the correlation between the human capital acquired by education and income level. Indeed in 2008 the medium wage of a high school graduate was $27,963; that of someone with an undergraduate degree was $48,097; and that of someone with a professional degree (MD or MBA) was $87,775 (Rajan 24).

Second, even though, education is society's way to increase human capital, education is faltering in recent American history. Thus, the US is falling behind 12 other rich countries in four-year-college graduation rates. College graduation rates for young men born in the 1970s were not higher than for those born in the 1940's. Finally, whereas Americans increased their years of schooling from 1930 to 1980 by 4.7 years they increased it from 1980 to 2005 by only 0.8 years (Rajan 25).

Third, Rajan argues that education has additional benefits. It has intrinsic value and allows us to do more refined things. Furthermore, level of education is correlated with taking better care of one's own health, with less participation in criminal activities and greater participation in both civic and political matters (Rajan 26).

Rajan now connects his argument about the importance of education with the growing income gap and argues that in conjunction they threaten the American dream. He summarizes that connection in the following beautiful paragraph in which he also develops the threatening possible consequences:

---

[12] Rajan seems to be following what he considers the majority opinion in the US, which is not opposed to income inequality, but insists on equality of access and opportunity for all, and especially access to quality education. The absence of this equality is seen as a violation of economic freedom. As actions to restore equal opportunity would take time and in the absence of a consensus on redistribution policies, including through taxation, the route chosen and agreed upon by politicians was easier credit, in particular to make housing more affordable.

> As more and more Americans realize they are simply not equipped to compete, and as they come to terms with their own diminished expectations, the words *economic free-dom* do not conjure open vistas of unlimited opportunity. Instead, they offer a nightmare vision of great and continuing insecurity, and growing envy as the have-nots increasingly become the have-nevers. Without some change in this trend, destructive class warfare is no longer impossible to contemplate (Rajan 30).

In his analysis Rajan thus sees that the growing income gap and the faltering education system are on the verge of destroying the American dream. Here I want to make a connection between Rajan's and Reich's analyses of the current economic crisis and my own more general analysis of economic reality. Among the domains for which I see an important role for the government by which to promote economic prosperity is what I call a "well functioning social contract." As part of such a social contract I envision "some kind of equality or equal opportunity so that all feel recognized, feel that they have a stake in the economy and are ready to participate in a free market" (Chap. 3). Several studies have connected the great success of Singapore and other Asian Tigers to such a "well functioning social contract."[13]

If it is true that the increasing gap in income combined with a faltering education system was threatening the American dream, which I like to refer to as the implicit American "social contract," it is no wonder that both Reich and Rajan look towards the political domain to see what the political actors did to salvage the American dream and thus to restore the implicit American contract.

Reich, who was part of the Clinton administration reports that the Clinton administration could only do frustratingly small things such as raise the minimum wage, guarantee workers time off for family and medical reasons, provide access to college for the poor, and expand the refundable tax credit for low-income earners (Reich 51). He does report that a grand deal was made between Clinton and Alan Greenspan in which Clinton agreed to reduce the federal budget deficit and Greenspan lowered the interest rates (Reich 51). This combined with a favorable moment in the business cycle promoted economic growth by the late 1990s.

Both Reich and Rajan mention the process of deregulation of Wall Street (Reich 56; Rajan 33) and mention it as a factor in the disproportionate growth of the financial sector (Rajan 142). Alarmingly, "between 1997 and 2007, finance became the fastest-growing part of the U.S. economy. The gains reaped by financial executives, traders, and specialists represented almost two-thirds of the growth in gross national product. By 2007, financial and insurance companies accounted for more than 40 % of American corporate profits and almost as great a percentage of pay, up from 10 % during the Great Prosperity" (Reich 56–57).

---

[13] For Singapore see Ghesquiere. For the other Asian Tigers see Campos and Root and World Bank 1997. Reich makes the same argument for the American period of Great Prosperity from 1947–1975 writing that "the basic bargain had ensured that the pay of American workers coincided with their output. In fact, the vast middle class received an increasing share of the benefits of economic growth" (Reich 51).

Rajan gives both the Clinton and Bush administration credit for seeing that something had to be done to keep the American dream alive. He documents the efforts by both administrations to restore or keep alive the American dream by providing cheap credit to buy homes. Thus he writes that in "2000, the Clinton administration dramatically cut the minimum down payment required for a borrower to qualify for an FHA guarantee to 3 %, increased the maximum size of mortgage it would guarantee, and halved the premiums it charged borrowers for the guarantee" (Rajan 37).[14] The administrations could make use of two government sponsored corporations: Fannie Mae and Freddie Mac.

Here Rajan makes the next step in his argument. He points out that Fannie Mae and Freddie Mac were the "government-supported private firms hungry for profits, and [they had] a weak and pliant regulator [which] proved disastrous" (Rajan 35). The Clinton administration increased the requirement to make low-income lending from 42 % of assets of those agencies in 1995 to 50 % in 2000 (Rajan 35–36). The Bush administration increased the requirement in 2004 to 56 % of assets (Rajan 38). On top of that the Clinton administration lowered the requirement for FHA guarantees to a down payment of 3 % while increasing the maximum seize of the mortgage and lowering drastically the premiums for the guarantee (Rajan 37). The push by the Clinton and the Bush administrations were not without effect. In 1997 Fannie Mae, Freddie Mac and the FHA did subprime lending of about $85 billion which became between $300 and $400 billion a year between 2003 and 2007. For 2007 this was 70 % of the market. Put in another way, in 2008 these three entities were exposed to $2.7 trillion in subprime and Alt-A loans, which was about 59 % of total loans of this kind. Cheap and easy money for the housing market was thus up to 2007 an effective way to keep the American dream alive notwithstanding the growing income gap between the very rich and the rest of society, particularly the less well off.

The next question in the puzzle is where all the money for these housing loans came from. Here we need to understand creative banking. As part of the combined thinking of both the US government and the Federal Reserve, where the Government wanted low interest for housing and the Federal Reserve was interested in low interest to promote economic growth, the price and return of money in the US was cheap. US investors were looking for higher returns and found that abroad. On top of that the US had consistently a large trade deficit. The US dollars were thus flooding into other countries. The Central Bankers of other countries wanted to avoid a devaluation of the dollar which would make the products of their own countries less competitive. There was thus great pressure to invest in dollar denominated instruments. By means of new instruments, American Banks and Financial Institutions rose up to the occasion. The use of cheap and easily available mortgage money created many assets which were used to create

---

[14] Bush made an enthusiastic connection between the American dream and home owning (Rajan 37).

asset-backed securities. Several risky steps were made which together created the possibility and even the likelihood of a financial collapse.

First, AAA rated securities were created from more risky underlying assets in two steps. One, many risky assets were combined in a diversified manner. Thus, if securities bundle assets of many states then a Katrina like disaster in a couple of states would be spread over securities tied to many states and the potential loss would be only a percentage of the loss if the assets were all from states hit by Katrina. Similarly, the collapse of one or another industry with the resulting unemployment and therefore inability for some workers to pay their mortgage would lead to a diminished percentage loss of the bundled assets as long as not all industries collapsed or as long as not all states were hit by such industry collapse. Two, the diminished liability was then "tranched" by slicing the bundled assets in securities with lesser or greater seniority. Greater seniority meant that your security did not need to absorb any losses of the underlying assets until junior securities had absorbed all the losses they could, i.e., for the full value of their security. Thus, tranched securities were so structured that all risk first hits the most junior slice of the security which then was given the highest return. The miracle of this asset-backed securities was that even the most senior slices paid a higher return than, say, similarly rated corporate bonds (Rajan 135). These instruments were therefore very attractive for the foreigners holding some of the many dollars residing in foreign hands because of the huge US deficit.

Second, many American financial institutions themselves held on to such newly created attractive securities but they did it with short term financing including overnight market financing.[15]

Third, the creators of these new securities insured the remaining risk with AIG (American International Group). Thus, the newly created securities seemed well thought out. Rajan helps us to concentrate upon the minute, almost hidden risk which was nevertheless there given the weakness of the underlying assets. This risk is called, in technical terms, the tail risk, i.e., the risk which occurs in the tail of the probability distribution (Rajan 137). The tail risk was, however, much more of a risk than generally accepted.[16] First, there was the fact that much of the weakness of the underlying assets had been hidden, sometimes even fraudulently. Second,

---

[15] "As of 2007, the five major investment banks—Bear Stearns, Goldman Sachs, Lehman Brothers, Merrill Lynch, and Morgan Stanley were operating with extraordinarily thin capital. By one measure, their leverage ratios were as high as 40 to 1, meaning for every $40 in assets, there was only $1 in capital to cover losses. Less than a 3 % drop in asset values could wipe out a firm" (Conclusions of The Financial Crisis Inquiry Report, XIX). "At the end of 2007 Bear Stearns had $11.8 billion in equity and $383.6 billion in liabilities and was borrowing between $50 and $70 billion in the overnight market (Conclusions of The Financial Crisis Inquiry Report, XIX–XX).

[16] Rajan points out that the financial actors knew about the so-called tail risk and created expressions for it, like: "the Acapulco Play, IBG (I'll be gone if it does not work), and, in Chicago, the O'Hare Option (buy a ticket departing from O'Hare International Airport: if the strategy fails, use it; if the strategy succeeds, tear up the ticket and return to the office)" (Rajan 139).

there was the fact that paying mortgages was dependent upon home owners being able to refinance their homes which had increased in price whenever the owners could not pay the mortgage. Third, financial institutions rewarded employees who were able to create instruments that provided higher than benchmark returns and removed risk managers who worried (Rajan 136, 141, 145).[17] Hence, employees were rewarded for not taking into account tail-risks. Fourth, regulators accepted the official risk assignment of the securities rather than the one signaled by the market. Hence, they allowed the lower capital requirements and thus encouraged the banks to invest in these kinds of securities (Rajan 151–152). Fifth, some members of the financial world did see the possibility that the tail-risk could explode because systemic factors in the economy–such as stagnant, or even decreasing, house prices were seen as possibl. Crucial members of the financial world made the calculation that in the case of a systematic explosion of the risk the government would have to step into save the whole economy. Hence, return for risky investment was rewarded and the calculation was made that losses of such risky investment, if they came, would be borne by someone else: the government, i.e., society as a whole.

Lastly, we need to point out that in the US the weak safety net under conditions of jobless recoveries and its political cost led to expansionary fiscal and financial policies following the 2001 recession. They were a factor contributing to the financial crisis of 2007–2008 as they promoted excess spending and by prolonged low interest rates pushed up asset prices and increased the taking of financial risk.

On September sixth the US took over Fannie Mae and Freddie Mac. On September fifteenth Lehman brothers filed for bankruptcy protection. On September sixteenth AIG accepted a bailout by the US. These facts showed that the tail risk had exploded. Banks were not certain which other bank might fail. Hence, lending between banks froze. Thus we see how a financial crisis caused a recession.

Rajan argues that a recession has different consequences in Europe than in the US. In Europe there exists in many countries a more generous, more long lasting and more flexible unemployment system. Employees can go on unemployment benefits for 1–3 days per week. Hence, European companies tend to keep their employees even in recession. As a consequence, European employees are willing to acquire non-transferable knowledge, i.e., knowledge applicable to the company they work in. In this environment, characterized as a system relying on long-term relationships not only with employees but with suppliers, bankers and customers as well, changes and improvements in business plans and actions are incremental (Rajan 89). In the US, firms work much more at arm's length. A crisis is used to restructure and workers are laid off. The reorganized firms in their ruthlessness achieve new efficiencies (Rajan 91–92). This new efficiencies allow the use of less workers. The US has seen in a series of recent recessions the phenomenon that factories start making big profits but unemployment remains high (Rajan 14).

---

[17] Benchmark return is the average return of similar securities.

5.6 Philosophical Interpretation of the 2007–2008 Crisis and the Ensuing Recession

Once the recession started in the US new categories of merit goods made themselves felt.[18] First, the US has a weaker safety net than many European countries. Indeed, US unemployment benefits are lower and of shorter duration (Rajan 93). Second, health insurance is substantially more expensive for private individuals because the US tax code subsidizes health insurance provided by the employer (Rajan 87). Unemployment then means either no health insurance or substantially more expensive insurance costs at a moment when income has dropped severely. The above mentioned two facts made the American population more anxious than in countries where there was a stronger safety net and universal health care. Furthermore, the prolonged unemployment rate after economic activity picked up after the latest recessions makes the anxiety even greater. Meager and short term unemployment benefits were tolerated in an economy where recessions were of short duration and where high unemployment rates were of short duration as well. The existing safety net was not appropriate for the changed economic fact of long term high unemployment rates. The weak short-term safety net was experienced as a broken social contract. Under these conditions American politicians felt great pressure to do things and to do things quickly. Pressure to make quick political decisions to deal with complex economic realities is not a guarantee for making the right decisions. The Obama administration was able to pass a stimulus package as recommended by Keynesian economics. But, as the widely respected journalist, Elizabeth Drew, wrote:

> The bill that came before Congress was a sprawling hodgepodge of proposals, as Democrats jumped at the chance to put in provisions, of varying soundness, that hadn't stood a chance for eight years. […] Obama and his advisers also seized the opportunity to put in the bill "down payments" on some of the President's priorities. Among these were funds for developing alternative energy; weatherizing buildings; updating school libraries and laboratories; building an electric grid to transmit new forms of energy; expanding broadband services; and providing funding for the computerization of health records—or Health Information Technology—an idea that had been around for many years but had

---

[18] The area of merit and demerit goods can give rise to a fundamental misconception: i.e., the idea that the government may intervene with everything in the economy and that such intervention has no limits. It is my view, however, that there are areas in the economy where the government unavoidably has to play a role such as in property specification and regulation of competition, credit creation and quality of many products. It is also my view that the role of the government can be wise or unwise. Hence, merit and demerit good actions must have solid reasons. These reasons limit the right for government intervention. Finally, it is also my view that the idea of merit and demerit goods is the way in which we see the conflict between capitalism and democracy work itself out (Rajan 18). This conflict can lead to felicitous and efficient outcomes or it can lead to deplorable outcomes. But the categories of merit/demerit goods provide a conceptual tool to reflect on dramatic aspects of capitalism like the events of 1929 and 2007–2008. In my view, Rajan makes deftly use of several categories of merit goods in his analysis of the 2007–2008 crisis and its aftermath.

foundered on questions of how to make the computers compatible and to ensure the privacy of electronic records. (Daschle had wanted it in the bill as a way to save health care money in the long run.)

It was a stretch to claim that all of the measures put in the bill would stimulate the economy (Drew 2).[19]

On top of that the US economy is both an export economy and an import economy absorbing the excess supply of a group of sizable export dependent economies. There was a world-wide recession. Thus the US faced limited opportunities to boost its exports as domestic demand in the export dependent countries remained constrained. Hence the size of US imports is unduly large and that of its exports unduly small. Other countries saw the quandary the US was in. Aware that the US was under great pressure to engage in expansionary policies from which they will benefit through the spillover effects, other countries which were reluctant or, because of their export dependency, unable to quickly respond to recessions could afford to take less forceful action than had the US not been under the compulsion to act early and forcefully. As a result the US was compelled to support a disproportionate burden in turning the world economy around (Rajan 100 and 118–119). Nevertheless, in contrast with the recession of 2001, faced with the Great Recession after the financial crisis of 2007–2008 many countries, including China, engaged in fiscal stimulus programs and adopted expansionary monetary policies thereby contributing to global economic recovery (For China, IMF 2010a 4–5 and 8–9; globally IMF 2009 71–83)

5.6.1 Conclusion

I like to gather the socio-political dimensions of the latest financial crisis and the recession that followed it.

The first phenomenon stressed by several authors is that the widening income gap between the very rich and the rest of society created a threat to the American dream.

The second phenomenon is that education has become more and more correlated with income. Education at all levels in the US is losing its power to equalize. Hence education is not able to restore the belief in the American dream.

The third phenomenon is that both democrats and republicans felt the need to restore the American dream by providing cheap money to buy homes.

The fourth phenomenon is that a number of facts promoted great increase in financial activity. The rich had money to invest; the middle class and the poor increased their debt; the low interest in the US and the huge US deficit made many

---

[19] Still it is worth noting that despite various weaknesses in the stimulus program, indications are that its impact on output and employment was positive (Blinder and Zandi 2010, 17; IMF 2010b April, 44; IMF 2011, 1).

dollars available abroad; many sources looked at better returns; the US financial institutions created asset backed-securities using as underlying assets the subprime mortgages. Regulation and control of both subprime mortgages and the asset backed securities was lax or non-existing.

The fifth phenomenon is that, when the financial crisis created a recession, the US faced both a weak safety net and a lack of universal health care. These two facts threatened again the implicit social contract. American politicians were pressed to act. They did so inefficiently because of the need for speedy action and because of the need for political compromise. But the need to have results for an economy, relying both on export and imports, meant that the US needed to accept the undue burden to get the whole world economy back on its feet.

Let me now extract the ethical dimensions which I classify as merit good categories.

The most important ethical dimension present in the Reich-Rajan explanation of the financial crisis is the threat to the American dream and thus to the implicit social contract created by the widening income gap between the very rich and the rest of society.

Rajan makes again use of the threat to the implicit social contract when he explains the need of American politicians to act quickly to the recession. Here the social contract is threatened because in the US innocent sufferers of a recession are not protected by a strong safety net (generous and long lasting unemployment benefits) and by a universal health care.

Next, Rajan points to a relaxation of both regulation and enforcement of regulation of the banking sector.

Finally, Rajan points out that there was a lack of transparency in the creation of subprime mortgages and in the risks taken by the financial sector with mortgage backed securities.

We thus see that the Reich-Rajan analysis of the current financial crisis and the subsequent recession presents us with the need to do also a socio-political analysis of the economy. Such a socio-political analysis gives the government a series of ethical duties it must perform in order for there to be an efficient and human economy.[20] Reich-Rajan make use of seven of the eleven merit good categories by which I try to understand the legitimate functions of the government in an economy: breakdown of a well functioning social contract (gap in income distribution threatened American dream; lack of protection in a recession); a weak safety net; absence of universal health insurance; failing education system; lack of transparency; lack of proper banking responsibility to deal with the down turn in the economic cycles.[21]

---

[20] For a libertarian analysis of the financial crisis which does not look for solutions by government actions, see: Lomasky, 2011.

[21] The eleven categories are enumerated in footnote 4.

5.6.2 Post-Script

For the United States to address properly the above mentioned seven merit good categories a deep moral transformation of American thinking will be needed. To provide an idea of the magnitude of the task we only have to look at how current tax rates would have to change in order to diminish the income gap between the very rich and the rest of society. For 2010 the Federal top tax rate is 35 %. In the 1950's, the period called by Robert Reich, the Great Prosperity: 1947–1975, the top income tax rate was, under President Eisenhower, 91 % (Reich IX and 49). This represents an enormous difference in top tax rate. Even the more modest proposal by Robert Reich of a top rate of 55 % looks draconian within the current mood of the country.

We can point to the enormous opposition to Obama's healthcare, the strong opposition to educational reform, the reluctance to extend unemployment benefits before the grand and expensive compromise during the final weeks of 2010 and the weakness of the financial reforms in which the problem of too big to fail was not addressed in order to remind us that properly implementing merit good categories will be an enormous task. The American form of late capitalism faces enormous challenges.

References

Blinder AS, Zandi M (2010) Stimulus Worked. http://www.imf.org/external/pubs/ft/fandd/2010/12/Blinder.htm. Finance & Development, pp 14–17

Campos JE, Root H (1996) The key to the Asian miracle. Brookings Institute, Washington

Drew E (2009) Thirty days of Barack Obama. www.nybooks.com/articles/22450. New York Review of Books, March 26

Financial Crisis Inquiry Commission (2011) The financial crisis inquiry report. US Government Printing Office, Washington

Ghesquiere H (2007) Singapore's success. Engineering economic growth. Thomson, Singapore

Head JG (2008) Review of: Wilfried Ver Eecke, an anthology regarding merit goods. Purdue University Press, West Lafayette, 2007. http://www.amazon.com/Anthology-Regarding-Merit-Goods-Unfinished/dp/1557534284/ref=sr_1_3?s=books&ie=UTF8&qid=1343652299&sr=1-3&keywords=Ver+Eecke

IMF (2009) Country and regional perspectives. In: World economic outlook. http://www.Imf.Org/External/Pubs/Ft/Weo/2009/01/Pdf/C2.>. IMF, Washington, April, pp 63–106

IMF (2010a) Country and regional perspectives. In: World Economic Outlook. http://www.Imf.Org/External/Pubs/Ft/Weo/2010/01/Pdf/Text.Pdf, IMF, Washington, April, pp 43–68

IMF (2010b) People's Republic of China: 2010 article IV consultation-staff report http://Www.Imf.Org/External/Pubs/Ft/Scr/2010/Cr10238.Pdf. IMF, Washington, p 37

IMF (2011) US fiscal policy and the global outlook. http://www.Imf.Org/External/Np/Speeches/2011/010811.Htm. IMF, Washington

Keynes JM (1965) The general theory of employment, interest, and money. Harcourt, Brace & World, Inc, New York

Kumhof M, Rancière R (2010) Inequality, leverage and crises. IMF Working Paper WP/10/268

Lomasky L (2011) Liberty after Lehman brothers. Soc Philos Policy 28:135–165

Musgrave RA (1959) The theory of public finance, Musgrave at Michigan University. McGraw-Hill Book Company, New York

Rajan RG (2010) Fault lines. How hidden fractures still threaten the world economy. Princeton University Press, Princeton

Reich RB (2010) Aftershock. The next economy and America's future. Alfred A. Knopf, New York

Reinhart CM, Rogoff KS (2008) This time is different: a panoramic view of eight centuries of financial crises. NBER Working Paper No. 13882, April 16, pp 1–123

Reinhart CM, Rogoff KS (2009) This time it is different: eight centuries of financial folly. Princeton University Press, Princeton

Schumpeter JA (1969) The theory of economic development. Oxford University Press, Oxford

Stiglitz JE (1999) Whither reform? Ten years of the transition. World Bank, Washington, pp 1–32

Stiglitz JE (2012) The price of inequality. How today's divided society endangers our future. W. W. Norton & Co, New York

Ver Eecke W (2007) An anthology regarding merit goods. The unfinished ethical revolution in economic thought. Purdue University Press, West Lafayette

Ver Eecke W (2008) Ethical dimensions of the economy. Making use of Hegel and the concepts of public and merit goods. Springer, Berlin

World Bank (1997) World development report 1997: the state in a changing world. Oxford University Press, New York

Chapter 6
Conclusion

Abstract I here survey the content of the book. In Chap. 2 I demonstrate that Adam Smith argued for allowing the self-interest of individuals to be the motor of the new efficient free market economy. Adam Smith saw a modest role for the government to deal with roads and education. I argue that this insight leads to the need to develop the concepts of public and merit goods. I develop those concepts in Chap. 3. In Chap. 4 I develop eleven domains where the government has a regulatory function. I call them the eleven categories of merit goods. In the last chapter I show, on the basis of the writings of Rajan, Reich and Reinhart & Rogoff, that the financial crisis 2007–2008 and the subsequent recession can be explained by deficient governmental actions in seven of the eleven merit good categories.

Keywords Adam Smith • Self-interest • Individuals • Competition • Public goods • Merit goods • Eleven categories of merit goods • Financial crisis 2007–2008 • Role of government • Regulation of banks

In this book we learned from Adam Smith the conceptual framework necessary to evaluate the health of the free market economy. Smith taught us that needless government interference in the economy should be replaced by free competition between individuals and groups of individuals. He argued that their competitive self-interest would work, as by an invisible hand, for a miraculously efficient economy. Adam Smith also argued that intelligent government help was necessary for dealing with public goods. Finally, Adam Smith demonstrated that the government in some cases needs to interfere with the wishes of individuals and groups. I argued that he hereby introduced the reasoning associated with the concept of merit good as introduced by Richard Musgrave. We claim that Adam Smith's argument for the regulations of the banking system is an argument for the fact that the government has to take the necessary steps to guarantee the wellbeing of the whole economic system, even if that involves the limitation of some freedom by some economic actors.

In Chap. 3 we analyzed the modern conception of public goods and merit goods. In Chap. 4 we argued for eleven domains in which the government needs to take actions to guarantee the possibility of efficient economic activity that is also moral.

W. Ver Eecke, *Ethical Reflections on the Financial Crisis 2007/2008*,
SpringerBriefs in Economics, DOI: 10.1007/978-3-642-35091-7_6,
© The Author(s) 2013

In Chap. 5 we demonstrated that the financial crisis of 2007–2008 and the subsequent recession can be greatly explained by the deficient provision of merit good decisions in seven of our eleven categories. We relied there upon the writings of highly respected authors in political economy such as Rajan, Reinhart and Rogoff and Reich. We thus believe that our philosophical reflections on the necessary framework of a healthy economy can contribute to the ideas necessary to avoid future such financial crises. We believe also that macro-economic theory and public finance might benefit from the study of the important domains where we argue that merit good decisions need to be made.

Printed by Publishers' Graphics LLC